THE
TRANSACTION

Other books by Chris Creamer

Running on Empty
(with Dr. Marc Cooper)

Valuocity 3
(with Dr. Marc Cooper)

THE TRANSACTION

Chris Creamer

Sahalie Press

Copyright 2015

THE TRANSACTION

Published by Sahalie Press
Woodinville, Washington

ISBN: 978-1500565268

Printed in the U.S.A.

First Edition, 2015

Editing by Matt King

PREFACE

Life is a coin.
You can spend it any way you wish.
But you can only spend it once.
Spend wisely.
~ P.L.W. Martin

How will you spend your coin? That's the question. Often, too many of us fret over the "big purchase" —an around-the-world cruise, tickets to the Super Bowl, the vacation home in Malibu. Yet, every day, moment-by-moment we engage in small, seemingly insignificant transactions: with a supermarket cashier, a bank teller, a waitress, another driver, a salesperson.

What if the sum of these transactions was the "big purchase"—the legacy—we could create with our lives? If we put forth our most authentic self in each and every transaction, every daily interaction, what would that mean to each of us personally? What would it mean to the various communities in which we live, work and play?

The Transaction provides a window into that world of authentic transactions and personal service that exceeds expectations. This is a fable of family, loss, struggle, hope and redemption—one typical transaction after another, starting with a cup of coffee.

Life is a coin... You can only spend it once.

PROLOGUE

The coin glowed as bright as the sun high in the sky. The young boy stared with disbelief into his palm as the old man stood tall above him, his simple cotton robe and grey hair flowing gently in the breeze.

"For me? Truly?" the boy asked.

"For you. Truly," the elder one replied. "Did you not render me a great service? Did you not restore to me my flock?"

The boy nodded. "Yes. But the sheep would've found their way home."

"Not all. The wolves have become thick of late and they hunger as never before."

"I know their hunger." The boy lowered his eyes.

"So do we all, but you returned my flock and not one is missing. You have served me and yourself well."

"And the coin is mine? To keep? It is the gold of the emperor. I have never held such."

The old man bent to one knee, looking the young boy in the eye. "The coin is but a token, a symbol. A measure of gold. It is the clasped hands upon it that reveal its value. This coin you hold is an agreement. A compact. A covenant. A trust."

He held out a hand to the boy. The boy looked from the coin to the outstretched hand. He offered his own uncertainly. The old man grasped the boy's hand with both his and shook firmly. The boy responded, gripping the wizened palms, feeling an unusual sense of strength, a rightness he barely comprehended.

Smiling, the old man stood up to his full height. "It is a mighty thing to trade honestly and serve others. A handshake is that promise. It will last longer than the tombs of our rulers. Remember that, young one, and you will flourish. Wolves may seem strong, but they are self serving and cannot be trusted – and thus are weak in ways that we are strong."

The boy shielded his eyes as the old man pointed to the sky and bade him farewell, "We are all small beneath the vastness of the heavens. Only together, hand-in-hand, do we thrive. Be fair and be well, young one."

The boy watched as the old man walked away, dust rising from his footsteps. He clasped the coin tightly in his small, rough hands, considering the faith simply built in one afternoon shepherding lost sheep, wondering what a life of this could mean.

He took a last thoughtful look at the coin before slipping it into his tunic's inner pocket. The weight of the coin and the elder's words made a difference in his step, in his entire bearing, as he turned and headed home.

Dust swirled in impossible directions as he scanned the road ahead. His feet were heavy, sluggish, yet he knew he had to make a decision, choose a direction, do something. The wind and dust picked up energy and he was further engulfed by churning darkness and growing angst.

As he spun around to get some bearing on where he had come from, the air around him gelled. His body felt thick and unresponsive. He tried to yell for help, but as he strained to speak the wind blew even harder. Frozen upon that endless road his fear escalated and his indecision enveloped him.

Nathan shivered hard and woke.

The dream. Again. He pulled the blanket tight around his shoulders attempting to stem the helpless chill the dream always left behind. His wife, Jillian, rolled away from him and resumed her steady breathing. Nathan found himself holding his breath. Slowly he let it out, his entire body sinking into the mattress.

The dream had unnerved him the past several months and robbed him of much needed sleep. Nathan didn't need Freud to analyze this dream. He owned a small business which was teetering on the brink. And he wasn't sure how to find help, get answers and move forward. The dream was pretty straightforward. He was stuck, the path around him was unclear and he knew that if he didn't do something, and soon, he would be going down with the ship.

Based on experience, it'd be a while before he could get back to sleep, so Nathan gingerly bunched up the pillow under his head and began thinking about windows. Focusing on the tangible parts of the work gave him some respite from the growing anxiety about the future of his business.

It was a perfect, blue autumn morning in Woodinville as Nathan entered Seven Coins Coffee. He wasn't surprised by the overstuffed chairs, iron floor lamps with fanciful shades and eclectic collection of worn wooden tables and chairs that bespoke a folksy charm and comfort. After all, Woodinville is 'wine country,' home to over 100 wineries and tasting rooms.

What *was* surprising and what had brought Nathan inside was that the shop existed at all. On his way to work, he had stopped to see what manner of proprietor had either the courage or utter lack of business sense to open a coffee shop in the same strip mall as a Starbucks. Even in Woodinville, near caffeine-crazed Seattle, why would anyone want to go head to head with the green mermaid?

As a regular at the neighboring franchise, Nathan wanted to see for himself. His first impression was a good one. He liked the look and feel of the shop. Comfortable and uncomplicated. But Nathan had his doubts that the cozy setting would be enough to sustain it.

Even at this early hour, though, the place was hopping. Newness or novelty could explain that. But would it last? As a small business owner, he wrestled with these concerns more and more as the economy remained frustratingly stingy, and uncertain.

Opening a business in this economic climate took guts and he gave the owner credit for that. Nathan scanned the interior wondering who he or she might be. The staff looked fairly young; but everyone was looking younger to Nathan these days. Fifty-four didn't feel particularly old, but the fresh-faced, smooth-skinned baristas behind the counter made him wonder where time had gone. How had he negotiated childhood to middle age so fast? Steeped in his reflection, he mindlessly reached for his wallet.

"Whoa!" came a cry from behind. Nathan stiffened as he felt someone graze his elbow and turned to see who he'd brushed into. A woman in an apron emblazed with coffee beans was side stepping past him.

"Sorry!" Nathan exclaimed.

"Not to worry," the woman dismissed his apology with a kindly wave and a smile. "We've just opened and I don't mind dodging customers. That's for sure."

"Of course," Nathan said returning her smile.

Nathan studied the woman for a moment. She was fairly tall, medium build with auburn hair and a round, sunny face. She looked to be in her mid-forties.

Definitely older than the baristas, Nathan thought, so he took a stab. "Are you the owner?"

She smirked. "Uh, yup. You're looking at the crazy one who dared to open a coffee shop a stone's throw from Starbucks."

Nathan chuckled. "I have to admit that's the main reason I came in this morning. I usually get my coffee over there and I was curious about the new coffee shop on the block. Pretty gutsy move."

"Oh, I heard all that from my friends, family and my banker. But," she leaned in, "I've got a vision."

Seeing the twinkle in her eye, Nathan took the bait, "OK, so what's your vision? I'm a business owner myself and am always interested in what drives other business owners." He tried not to allow the fear he had about his own business surface in the question.

"You don't own a coffee shop do you?"

"No, no." Nathan shook his head. "I manufacture custom windows. Winning Windows. We do design work and fabrication a few blocks down the road."

"Well, in that case," she said, "from one non-competing small business owner to another, it's about making personal connections; that's what matters to customers. Big surprise, eh?"

Nathan nodded. "Well, I'm pretty sure Starbucks has a vision. But if you're willing to go toe-to-toe with them, it'll be interesting to see how your vision works against a corporate giant."

"Sure. That *is* the big question. But the Starbucks website says they set out to be a different kind of company. One that not only celebrated coffee and the rich tradition, *but also brought a feeling of connection.* And I think they are struggling with that vision."

She offered Nathan her hand. "I'm Annette Florence."

"Pleased to meet you, Annette. I'm Nathan Perkins."

She shook his hand warmly. "Glad to meet you, Nathan. I hope you enjoy your coffee."

"I will. I like the atmosphere here, though I'm sure you need to get back to your work."

"Actually, Nathan, I'm doing the most important part of my work right now." Annette paused as she reached into her apron pocket. She withdrew a quarter-sized gold-colored coin and offered it to him. "I realize everyone has their own special vision, but this little token is really the foundation of mine."

Nathan took the token and studied it. Both sides of the metal coin had a stamped image of two hands clasped in a handshake.

"What's it for?" Nathan asked.

"It's a philosophical statement, really," Annette mused. "It's why I picked this location to open my shop. This coin will determine if my philosophy of doing business, my whole way of thinking about people is right."

Nathan eyed her guardedly. "What do you mean?"

Annette looked past him towards the counter where the baristas were madly filling orders. "It's an involved story, but If you're really curious, feel free to come back sometime mid-morning or mid-afternoon when I have a bit more time. We can talk."

"Sure," Nathan said glancing over his shoulder. "I know you've got a crowd here." He offered the coin back to Annette.

She held up her hand. "Keep the coin. I'm nothing if not an evangelist for what I hope Seven Coins Coffee can do for small businesses. It'll remind you to come back and hear the story behind it. Thanks for giving us a try and have a wonderful day."

Nathan smiled politely and put the coin in his jacket pocket. "You've been very kind, and I haven't even had my coffee yet."

"Well, your day will get a whole lot better once you do," Annette said confidently as she strode towards the service counter.

After ordering and picking up his coffee, Nathan headed out to his car, taking a sip. It was rich, aromatic, satisfying. Very good coffee, he thought. And something more. Seven Coins had left him with a good vibe, a sense of comfort, and appreciation. Ironically, way more upbeat than his usual visit to Starbucks.

As he searched in his jacket for his car key, he felt the coin Annette had given him. He took it out and looked at it again. A handshake. He unlocked his car and sat in the seat sipping his coffee, thinking about the coin, and feeling a bit like he was leaving a friend's house.

Nathan's sense of well-being began to recede as he pulled into the employee parking lot of Winning Windows. He turned off the engine and sat looking up at the company sign.

In some capacity, he'd worked here his entire adult life. Some thirty-five years. Summers in high school and college doing fabrication in the factory, then getting into the sales side, and, after getting his business degree and becoming a CPA, he'd joined the company as their lead accountant.

Twelve years ago he bought the business. Nathan Perkins, owner and proprietor of Winning Windows. He currently had seventeen full-time employees and a half dozen part-time workers when things got busy. Which, unfortunately, hadn't been the case for a while.

In fact, Winning Windows had seemed more like *Waning Windows* the last several years. The sluggish economy, especially in construction, had left a lot of his employees complaining. Nathan had renegotiated contracts, benefits and hours to keep everybody on board. He'd put some of his full-time staff on part time, and let part-time staff go. It was either that or close the doors...never mind the windows!

It had been hard, but he'd done what he had to do, and business was creeping along, though sales had been ominously flat the last few months. Morale was low and many of his employees were going through their day mechanically. Nathan was overwhelmed and at a loss for what to do to correct their course.

For most of the three decades Nathan had been at Winning Windows, he'd enjoyed coming to work. He liked designing, manufacturing and selling windows. They were tangible things that people valued. He especially loved doing residential or commercial remodels and seeing clients' faces brighten when they got their new windows.

Even better was following up with customers after a few months to ask about the impact on their energy bills. They'd generally rave about his triple-paned windows. It was very satisfying.

But he hadn't felt that same contentment in a while. Everything was more of a battle. Suppliers. Sales. Bills. The tentativeness of the general economy was certainly part of the problem, but so was his mindset. Nathan worried that he was losing his passion—and losing faith—in the business and his employees. The sense of creative adventure he'd once felt was ebbing away.

Lost. Stuck. Like in his dream. He wondered if he had wasted his talents, squandered the opportunity his father had put before him. Clearly that's how his father saw it and the thought troubled him. He hadn't followed in Dr. Danforth Perkins' footsteps. He'd strayed from that path.

His father had been a dentist, a very good one. Over many years of hard work, his father had built a successful practice. For decades he'd been a pillar in the Woodinville business community with a reputation as good as gold. He'd expected Nathan would jump at the chance to go to dental school and join him and eventually take over his practice.

Sadly, Nathan had zero interest in becoming a dentist, and he'd made the terrible mistake of once telling his father, *I don't want to look into people's mouths my whole life.*

Then and there, something changed between them. His father seemed to turn his attention to Nathan's younger brother, Garrett. Garrett followed happily and became a dentist, eventually inheriting Dr. Danforth's dental practice—and much of his goodwill. Garrett became the favorite. And Nathan felt like a disappointment.

At least, that's how Nathan saw it. The irony, of course, was that he and his father were very much alike. Both hard working and building their own businesses. Both very stubborn.

Both missing, Gloria. His mom and their mediator. She had died of breast cancer a dozen years before. That had sent Nathan and his dad drifting even further apart.

Gloria died during the time he'd been purchasing Winning Windows. What a hellish half year that had been. It was almost as if his father blamed him for her death. Without the calming, reasonable bridge that was their mother, his father had grown more withdrawn from Nathan, favoring Garrett at family gatherings and calling on him when he needed help.

And, boy, did their father need help now. At close to eighty, his health was declining. More and more his bad days outnumbered the good ones. In large part due to a minor stroke he'd suffered two years ago which left him with memory problems and a bit unsteady on his feet.

Dr. Danforth had wanted to continue living by himself, but the stroke convinced Nathan and Garrett that their father needed some kind of assisted living facility. Garrett had spearheaded the arrangements. As much as Nathan had wanted to help with the transition, he knew his involvement would make it more difficult for his father to accept.

Recently, the situation had changed again. His health seemed to be worsening. He was having more memory lapses. Garrett had done the lion's share of caring for their father, but was needing Nathan to check on their father more and more often.

Dr. Danforth tolerated Nathan's visits with cranky acceptance. Sometimes he'd get a stony stare from his father. Sometimes, the stare would be blank. More and more, though, his dad would mix him and Garrett up, sometimes berating Garrett for going into the window business and then asking Nathan how the dental practice was going.

It was sad and, deep down, Nathan knew the decline of his father's health and their long fractured relationship was also affecting his outlook on Winning Windows—and his optimism about the future in general.

He sighed heavily, as he got out of his car. It wasn't exactly dread he was feeling as he headed inside the factory; it was more a creeping malaise. He wished he could just chalk the bleak feeling up to it being Monday, but there was more to the story. He was rapidly becoming a failure as a son, as an owner and as a provider for his family.

As Nathan entered the showroom of Winning Windows, Gracie and Estevan were arguing. Nathan knew too well the familiar rhythm of their back and forth he-said-she-said disagreements. At times, he wanted to scream. What had before seemed like friendly competitive banter had escalated in the last few months into vapid quarrels over marketing strategies.

Gracie and Estevan had been such a good, productive team at one time, but that was when they'd had a sales manager. Unfortunately, with the sluggish economy, their sales manager had jumped ship to their main competitor: AMVIC Windows and Fittings. At the time, Gracie and Estevan maintained that they could handle the sales load between them, which for the most part they had. More and more, though, Nathan was noticing that they were becoming territorial and dismissive of each other.

They were both bright, hard working employees, but their bickering was one of the things that made Nathan's work less satisfying and more of a grind. He half-heartedly waved to them as he ducked into his office, where he hoped he could get his thoughts back on a more positive and productive track.

He was able to focus for about two hours before he realized he needed a "Foster fix" and meandered towards the assembly area. Winning Windows was comprised of two wings. The smaller wing held the showroom with samples of their products and materials as well as the sales office and his office. In the larger wing, the bulk of the fabrication took place in a somewhat cavernous space called the Skylight because Nathan had installed twenty skylights to provide more natural lighting and cut down on electricity bills. After all, they were a window company.

The Skylight was usually noisy, smelly and chaotic. And Nathan loved it. This is where he'd started thirty-five years ago as a gofer for the assemblers as well as cleaning up the vinyl and glass pieces leftover at the day's end. The bustle of the place had always made him feel like things were getting done, that he was helping to make things people wanted.

He put on safety glasses and hung a pair of ear muffs around his neck. He entered through two sets of double doors that separated the Skylight from the offices and showroom. Even though they weren't even close to working at full capacity, the assembly area was loud and busy. From the doorway, he watched the activity for a few moments, wondering if his employees were satisfied. Did they enjoy coming to work? Or was this just a job to most of them?

He observed intense frowns of concentration and short, clipped interactions. It had the aura of efficiency, but that was it.

Nathan went to the one person he thought could tell him. He walked over to the nearest assembly table where Foster, who had worked at Winning Windows ten years longer than Nathan, was spreading out the pieces for a large arched entryway window.

"How's it going, Foster?" Nathan asked, trying to sound as upbeat as possible.

Foster looked up from his work and nodded, shifting an ever-present toothpick from one side of his mouth to the other. "Going fine, Nathan. How about with you? You have a nice weekend? Anything up?"

"You know, just thinking about life, the universe and everything."

Foster grinned. "Well, that's what the boss has to do. I just have this window here to think about."

"Yeah, I guess you're a lucky man." Nathan smiled back and moved a step closer. "But do you feel lucky? I mean, coming here on a Monday morning and making windows, do you enjoy it?"

Foster lifted his safety glasses so they rested on the top of his head. "You still wrestling with that whole job satisfaction and happiness thing? Or is this about our conversation last month about more automation? I thought we talked that all through. You know I like what I do. And I don't think more machines will help us do it any better. We've got a good balance and we make an excellent product which I'm proud of. It's a good job—and you're a good boss. Though you're tending to the worrying side lately."

Nathan shrugged. "It's Monday. It's when I do my best worrying. Besides, I didn't sleep so well last night."

"Your dad?" Foster asked.

"Hard to say," Nathan replied. He'd confided in Foster about his father's declining health. "I'm sure Dad's health is part of it."

Nathan surveyed the other workers moving purposely around them. "I think I'm worried about everyone. There's so much uncertainty."

"Always is."

"Not like this."

Foster shrugged.

Nathan shrugged back. "Okay, I get it. I'll worry less – but will you let me know if you start to worry more?"

Foster lowered his safety glasses back over his eyes and clasped Nathan's shoulder. "Deal, Boss."

Nodding, Nathan smiled. He then walked over to check in with a few other employees. They were friendly and decently cheerful for a Monday, but none of them made Nathan feel as reassured as Foster had.

On his way back to his office, Nathan passed through the showroom as Gracie was showing a young couple with a toddler some of the window samples. The little boy was pressing his hand and face against each of the samples. The mother finally picked the child up, but not before Nathan caught Gracie rolling her eyes with disdain.

Gracie and Estevan were responsible for keeping the showroom models clean and sparkling, but Gracie needed to show more graciousness. The couple was a potential client and she couldn't take the chance of rubbing them the wrong way.

He was tempted to intervene right then, but the child began fussing in his mother's arms, exploding in a barrage of tears. The dad huddled around his wife and, just like that, they muttered apologies to Gracie who was looking grimly at the young boy flailing in his mother's arms. Then they were on their way out the door.

"Can you believe some people?" Gracie asked as Nathan approached. "Did you see that brat smearing his snot nose on all our windows? Some people don't know how to handle kids. Where are their manners?"

Like you rolling your eyes at that poor mom, Nathan wanted to say, but he bit it back. He didn't want to get into it with Gracie right then. Even though, his dad had advised him when he'd bought the business: "Nathan, if you step over the trash too many times, it'll bury you."

But, Nathan knew that if he got into it with her now, he would explode and the real message would be lost. Gracie needed to think about *her* manners, not the toddler's. She was the adult in the room. She could use a lesson or two of empathy.

Nathan suddenly thought back to what Annette, the owner of Seven Coins Coffee had said about her coin. She'd said she was putting her convictions about how people should conduct business into practice.

Retreating back to his office, Nathan dug the coin out of his jacket pocket. He looked at the simple image of the handshake and reflected on Gracie's interaction with the young couple in the showroom. As a salesperson, Gracie knew windows, their insulation values, as well as creative discounting and financing, but he wondered if she really knew people all that well.

Tapping Annette's coin on his desk, he looked at the clock. It was getting close to 11:00. With sudden decision, he grabbed his jacket, walked into the showroom and brusquely called to Gracie, "I'm taking an early lunch today. I'll be back about noon."

Gracie gave him a 'whatever' wave of a hand as she continued wiping down the floor samples with glass cleaner.

Whatever.

That was exactly the attitude bothering Nathan. It was exactly the opposite of what he'd felt in Seven Coins Coffee this morning. That feeling had been: *Welcome. You matter.* Not: *Whatever. I matter more than you.* Or: *Whatever, you only matter because I get paid to acknowledge you.*

As he went out to his car, Nathan took another look at the coin. He was hoping she had the time to tell him the story behind the coin. How she really expected to compete against Starbucks.

He needed help. Needed some answers on how to get unstuck. Get back his sense of direction. He was tired of feeling lost and adrift. If nothing else, he mused, another cup of coffee would keep his weary mind awake after having had such a restless sleep the previous night.

Nathan found it difficult to concentrate as he sat across from Annette. He felt uncomfortable, wondering if he was wasting Annette's time.

She was very polite when he'd asked if she had a free moment. Nathan had bought coffee and a decadent-looking macaroon and taken a seat. Annette joined him a few minutes later. He put the coin on the table as he took a drink.

"So, you want to know the story of the coin?" she asked a bit guardedly. "You sure don't waste any time getting at my business secrets."

Nathan smiled in spite of his apprehension. "Look at it this way: if your golden coin works as well selling windows as it does coffee, you'll be able to sell your secret for some real Krugerrands."

She smiled back and confessed. "This might sound strange, but opening my own shop isn't really about the money."

"That would explain why you chose a location right next to a Starbucks, then."

"Oh, I want to make money," Annette assured him, "and I *intend* to make money. But, that's not my underlying motivation. I could've stuck to my old job where I was making a comfortable living. For me, this whole endeavor is about value. What people really value.

"Our corporate culture is focused on growth and maximizing profits and the mantra is 'growth is good.' But growth has its own cost. You can get so caught up in winning that you lose the fundamental understanding that trade and commerce should be mutually beneficial. It's not about one side getting a better deal. It's about both sides gaining equitably. That's sustainable business. It's authentic—and when it's authentic, it should be personal.

"I know this might sound overly dramatic, but that authentic, personal aspect of doing business is why I opened Seven Coins. If you lose touch with looking customers and clients in the eye and shaking their hands, you can risk losing sight of your vision."

She paused and pointed to the clasped hands etched in the coin. "The handshake is such an ancient ritual of closing a deal. Each person agreeing to exchange something he or she possesses for something he or she values more. It's the basis for all economic activity: transactions.

"It's the fundamental stuff we do almost every day of our lives. I've done tens of thousands of transactions: babysitting, scooping ice cream, selling at a high-end boutique, trading bonds and cutting deals as a corporate vice president."

Nathan's eyes widened, and Annette's eyes narrowed at his reaction. "Does that surprise you? A former bond trader and corporate veep opening a coffee shop? I hope you're not thinking it's because I tanked when Wall Street did a few years ago, or that I cheated investors out of their 401Ks."

"Sorry, no," Nathan admitted. "It just seems quite a switch to go from high finance to the everyday running of a coffee shop."

"It is. But that's what I wanted. I was getting too far from *this*." She held the coin up. "I was missing authentic transactions: handshakes, smiles, interacting with customers and saying 'Thank You.' Seeing new people every day and feeling part of a community.

"When I took the time to reflect, to really think about what I value and what I wanted to do with the rest of my life, I discovered that my core values don't have much to do with corporate ideas of success like money and power. For me, it's about relationships. That's the foundation. If you cultivate and build solid relationships, life flourishes – and so can any business, one authentic transaction at a time."

Annette handed the coin back to Nathan. "Pretty simple, huh?" She laughed lightly.

"To you, maybe, Nathan responded. "You seem to have it all figured out. To me, your approach sounds much more complicated than building windows. I wouldn't know where to begin. It sounds time intensive."

Annette nodded. "It is, but people make time for what they value. It becomes a question of resource allocation. It's no different than a manufacturer like yourself investing in high quality materials and superior training for his employees – if you value a top-of-the-line finished product."

"Okay, that seems more straightforward."

"Straightforward, yes," Annette acknowledged. "But, it's not easy. Think about it for a second, Nathan. Getting in shape should be pretty straightforward for most people. Exercise consistently and eat the right foods. Pretty simple to understand, right? But, we Americans seem to find that simple rule hard to put into practice. Knowledge, knowing what to do, doesn't by itself change behavior. You've got to focus on people's habits to affect real change."

She gestured around the shop that was mostly empty at the moment. "Right now I could be doing lots of other things that are part of running my business, like prepping for the lunch crowd, developing marketing materials, checking on my employees, etc. But I'm choosing to talk with you. Because that is what the core of my business really is: creating the service, the kind of transaction we'll both remember and value."

Annette let that sink in and then asked, "What makes you feel best about running your company?"

It was a surprisingly easy question for Nathan. "You know, following up with customers and hearing how happy they are with our windows."

"Exactly. You derive a deep satisfaction from providing your customers with a great product and service. Notice what an exchange that is. Yes, money exchanged hands, but it is the mutual satisfaction that you remember and value."

She pointed to his half-empty latte. "The kind of business I want to run here is not just about the coffee you bought and the money I received. It's about the attention we give each other. The sense that we both matter. That's what I'm trying to instill in my employees. I want them to deeply internalize the feeling of a good transaction. One that is lasting and authentic.

"That's why I had the coins made. It's part of my employee training." She smiled and her eyes brightened. "Honestly, it's my plot to change the world. And I owe it all to a minister in Walla Walla."

"Walla Walla?" Nathan asked, knowing he was about to go deeper down the rabbit hole and intrigued at where it might take him.

"Yes. Walla Walla," Annette continued. "Close to twenty years ago, I went there to help set up financing for a new winery. The first Sunday of my stay, I attended the local Presbyterian church because that's a part of who I am.

"The minister was easily in his seventies, but he was animated and entertaining. The sermon was about how to treat our neighbors, people in our community, our families. Even now I remember he quoted Ephesians:

> *Be kind to one another, tenderhearted, forgiving one another."*

"But what really made an indelible impression was his message to the congregation before the collection offering.

"At the pulpit, he boldly told his congregation, 'I've known many of you for decades. You're generous people and you've supported this church and its programs in many ways. Today, instead of accepting your offering, we're passing out aluminum coins. I want you to spread wholesale goodness this coming week. Honor your values and the exchanges you have every day with those in our community. Give them your best. Let them know they matter. When you find someone who is making an exchange with you that is authentic and human, and from the heart, give them the coin. Explain to them what you're doing and why. So, this week I don't want your money, but next week I expect to hear your stories.'

"The offering plates were passed out, piled high with the coins and the energy amongst the congregation was palpable. They were smiling, talking to their neighbors, laughing. It was a grand experiment, I tell you.

"The following Sunday, the minister invited folks up to the microphone to share their stories. Dozens of hands went up as he asked for volunteers. There were many heartfelt stories that morning. Most of the congregation had reached out to make connections to people they interacted with every day, but often took for granted. When they had finished sharing their stories, the minister thanked them for their willingness to participate. He reminded his flock that they had the power to do good every day—which didn't mean they had to give away money—they could give of their spirit.

"He said they needed to keep being interested and willing to be involved in the lives of the people around them. To him, that was the essence of a healthy community and the only way humans were ever going to get a little heaven on earth.

"The amazing thing was the wave this one action set into motion. I gave my coin to a bagger at the Safeway. He just seemed to be genuinely enjoying his job and interacting with people in his line as well as the two lines to either side. I got something out of that. The woman ringing up my purchases, on the other hand, asked all the required questions. *How's your day? Did you find everything?* I assume they're 'required' questions because I hear them every time I pay for groceries at Safeway.

"Anyway, I heard stories about the coins all week at the winery, during meetings, as I ran errands, or saw them sitting on counters or cash registers. Those couple hundred coins probably reached several hundred people in the community, thousands maybe, as the stories got passed around to friends and family.

Annette paused again and looked wistfully around her coffee shop. "That minister's inspiration and the stories his parishioners told of the importance of everyday transactions in our lives sank deep into my soul. The simple truth of that experience has been percolating ever since."

Nathan chuckled, "And, twenty years later, that minister's idea *percolated* this coffee shop into existence."

"Yes," Annette smiled in agreement. "That Walla Walla minister gave his congregation a great lesson in how to make people matter. Every day. All the time. I think it's not only a beautiful life lesson. I believe it's also an excellent business model.

"So, the transaction coins are my way of teaching that lesson. And, though I know they will probably never replace Krugerrands, I think they could become a kind of currency for transforming a person's mindset about service to others."

Nathan thumbed the edge of the coin Annette had given him. "Yup. This probably won't replace 24 karat gold, but I think I catch your meaning. So, you give the coins to your employees to remind them to provide great customer service – or as a token when you've witnessed them provide outstanding service."

"I'm trying to take it a bit deeper than that," Annette explained. "I hand out seven coins when I hire a new employee. Their job is to give those seven coins away in a week: one coin for each authentic transaction they observe or take part in. That's how I want them to internalize this idea of genuine service. I think it becomes a whole lot easier to give great service when people matter to you. And people only matter to you if you take the time to get to know them. Establish a relationship on some level. That's what we ultimately value. Great salespeople have always known that.

"So, with the coins, I ask my employees to evaluate and reflect on the dozens of transactions they have each day and determine if any of them are worth a good, old-fashioned handshake."

"Wow. You know, Annette, that's kind of brilliant," Nathan remarked.

"Well, I don't know about brilliant, but I think it works. It's a way of helping my employees engage with customers. Not as a mindless ritual you get with some greeters in big box stores or an awkward parroting back of your name off the receipt at the check out register by the cashier at a supermarket chain. This is about meeting and serving fellow humans in your business. Making both parties feel a connection and a benefit from the interaction. I want my workers to think about transactions from both sides: as employees and customers."

For a moment, Nathan studied the golden coin. "But, how do you know if your employees are doing what you ask them to do with the coins?"

"I don't for sure," Annette admitted. "But we share stories at the beginning of each shift. It helps us calibrate and get closer to what we each think an authentic transaction feels like. It seems to be working – at least, they're coming back with interesting stories. They're not taking their day-to-day interactions with their fellow human beings for granted and I think that's a good step."

Nathan grinned and was quiet for a moment. "Thanks, Annette. You've given me a lot to think about, and I know you've got to get back to work...I mean, the other parts of your job. I appreciate the time you've given me, and if I were one of your employees I think I should be giving you this gold coin for a meaningful transaction." He offered it to her.

She shook her head. "Thanks. But, I think you'd better keep it. In fact," she dug into her apron and counted out six more coins and handed them to Nathan, "it strikes me that I'd like to see if you can give away seven coins. You've got a week to give away those seven tokens to folks you have a meaningful transaction with. I expect a full report by next Monday."

Momentarily caught off guard, Nathan stuttered, "Wait. I...I...don't need to do that. I think I've got the concept."

"Understanding the concept and seeing what it looks and feels like in practice are two different things," Annette countered. "You know, 'teaching a man to fish versus feeding a man a fish.' It's up to you, though, Nathan. Look on it as a down payment for learning my trade secret."

He hesitantly took the gold tokens and slid them into his jacket pocket. "I guess I'm accepting your mission *and* learning to fish," he said with a mock salute. "I just hope I don't mess it up. I don't want you to lose faith in your system because I screwed it up."

"Don't worry," Annette laughed lightly. "Nothing ventured, nothing gained. Remember, Nathan, lots of people sell things, but they don't always try to make the experience meaningful. I'm here to make a better world, one cup of coffee, one transaction at a time."

Nathan nodded thoughtfully and thanked her as she rose from the table. He slowly finished his coffee and macaroon, thinking about the seven coins in his pocket, wondering what he'd gotten himself into. Did the coins represent a possible treasure or a curse?

The rest of the afternoon dragged for Nathan. It wasn't that he didn't have things to do; he did. It was his growing preoccupation with Annette's gold coins. He eventually got up from his desk and went looking for evidence of the authentic, lasting transactions she had talked about.

One minute he'd heard Gracie and Estevan sharing a laugh in the showroom; the next minute they were bickering over the bid they were putting together for a big contractor building an apartment complex called Sunset Gardens. It was a major contract Nathan felt they needed, and he knew they were competing against AMVIC Windows who always looked to undercut their pricing.

Competing against AMVIC and other window manufacturers who were much bigger had driven Nathan to consider investing in automation. Machines cost a lot up front, but they would cut his production costs in the long run. He'd asked Foster to help him do an initial cost/benefit analysis and they'd both concluded they liked the flexibility and quality control that manpower gave them.

But as he thought about it, if they tried to compete with AMVIC on price, they were always certain to lose. If contractors were going to continue to go with the cheapest bid, then that's what they were going to get. *The cheapest product.* What Winning Windows offered was a promise of quality that would last for years vs. the upfront cost of coming in under budget.

When he walked over to the Skylight wing, it was like an ant colony. Dozens of ongoing interactions. It looked efficient. Was it friendly? Was it meaningful to his employees? Should it be? Nathan had his doubts about what Annette was really trying to accomplish. Maybe it could work in a small coffee shop, but in a large window factory? They were talking retail vs. wholesale, after all.

Dozens of interactions happened every day between people. How was that different from a meaningful transaction? He wished he'd thought to ask Annette. He toyed with the idea of stopping back by her coffee shop, but she had her own worries. And he didn't want to look like a stalker.

The phone rang and jarred him from his thoughts. His world got a bit bleaker when Nathan saw his brother's name on the phone's display. That wasn't usually a good sign. Nathan and Garrett got along well, but lately all their conversations revolved around their father and his troublesome health issues.

He picked up. "Hey, Garrett, what's up?"

"Dad's down, that's what's up," Garrett answered. "I just got a call from a nurse at Aurora. They say he seems somewhat depressed. He's not eating much and is acting lethargic."

"Do they think he's come down with something? A cold, the flu?"

"They don't think so," Garrett responded. "They don't know why he's taken this downturn, but one of us needs to go see him, and I can't tonight. Marcy's got a recital."

This is what it had come to with their father: which of them had something more important to do than to be at his side. He got it. In fact, he felt he owed

Garrett a lot for being the one his father most leaned on.

Though Dr. Danforth had christened Garrett the good son for following him into dentistry, Garrett had never abused that status with Nathan. He'd always tried to be a peacemaker between Nathan and their father. He just wasn't as successful as their mother had been.

Nathan hesitated. Being with his father was hard in a way he couldn't fully explain. Between them there was never any give and take. They were two blocks of solid ice chipping away at each other.

Finally, Nathan cleared his throat. "No problem. I'll go by on my way home. See if I can get him to eat something. Maybe, he'll think I'm you again and take a few bites."

Garrett laughed grimly. "It's a shame, isn't it? Poor guy. He was always so tough and sure of himself."

"He's still tough—and he's still sure," Nathan said. "His opinions haven't changed. He's just not always sure who he's talking to anymore."

"Yeah, well, sorry to throw this your way tonight, big brother. I appreciate you doing it," Garrett thanked him.

"Hey, you've been doing the heavy lifting with Dad for the last few years. My turn to step up."

"That's only because he wouldn't let you help, Nathan. Don't blame yourself for that. He was too set in his ways. He's one stubborn guy."

"We both know that," Nathan agreed. "Okay, I'll be checking in on him. You want me to call you later to give you an update?"

There was a brief pause. "Would you be able to swing by my office on your way in tomorrow? We can talk then. Plus, Dad's lawyer dropped off a few things for me to sign and I want to make sure you're okay with them."

"Sure. That'll work. I'll drop by about 7:30. Have fun at Marcy's recital. Tell her that her uncle is waiting to get an invitation someday."

Garrett laughed. "She gets nervous if too many people in the audience know her. I figure that in a year she'll be willing to have you and Jillian come listen. Then you'll be on the hook for another five or six years of recitals."

"Can't wait," Nathan promised. "Tell her that her cousin Lisa was the same way. Now she's a musical exhibitionist. She'd clarinet us to death if we gave her half a chance."

"Yup, the pendulum swings quickly when they get into their teens. Say 'Hi' to the family. Thanks again for doing Dad duty."

"No worries. See you tomorrow," Nathan said as he ended the call.

In spite of what he'd told his brother, Nathan was worried. Any time he spent with his father was mostly uncomfortable. With so much on his mind, he wondered how he was going to stay upbeat, which he needed to be. It was going to be a long evening, so he figured he'd better talk to Jillian and let her know the plan.

He called the floral department of the grocery store where she worked and she picked up on the first ring. 'Hey, hon. How's your day been?"

"OK," his wife answered. "Our suppliers actually gave us some decently fresh cuttings to work with, and only one zany request from a customer. What's up?" Since they always debriefed about their days during dinner, she knew he wouldn't be calling unless his schedule had changed.

"Garrett called and needs me to check on Dad. He's become more lethargic and isn't really eating according to the staff. I said I'd go over during his dinner and see what I can do."

"Sorry to hear that. Did they say if he had come down with something?"

"Garrett didn't know, but it's hard to say with Dad. Sometimes, he doesn't seem to be all there. Like he's slowly checking out."

"Yeah. It's not pretty, is it? You want me to come with you?" Jillian asked. "I can let Lisa know we won't be home for dinner."

"Thanks, Jilli, but you should go home. I'll take this shift. Considering we may be spending a lot more time there in the future, it's probably best to pace ourselves."

"I understand that, Nathan, but I also know how your dad can be. And I know my being there distracts him from harping on you."

"That's only when he thinks you're Mom," Nathan reminded her.

"Whatever works. If my being Gloria makes him happy, I'm glad to be mistaken for her."

Nathan chuckled into the phone. "You're a champ. Thanks for the offer, but I'll see how this goes. I may need a drink when I get home, though."

"I'll get out the good stuff for you."

"Thanks. I should be home between seven and eight. Hope the rest of your day isn't too zany."

Jillian giggled. "Me too. I'll tell you about the crazy request we had this morning when you get home. Be sure to get something to eat before you go see your dad and be sure to give him a hug—for me."

"I will. See you in a few hours." Nathan put down his phone and wondered if he would've thought to give his father a hug, if Jillian hadn't reminded him.

The sub shop Nathan stopped at on his way wasn't too crowded, but the sandwich makers were moving at a glacial pace and Nathan was really hungry. He realized about 4:00 that he hadn't eaten lunch. It was that second coffee at Seven Coins this morning that had knocked him off his routine. Now, his stomach was reminding him in no uncertain terms.

Impatiently, he waited as the employees mechanically assembled the orders of each customer. Maybe it was efficient. The price of fast food. Surprisingly, Nathan made a connection to what Annette had said about the nature of a transaction. Value for value.

He hadn't chosen this sub shop for a dining experience. He needed something to eat—and fast. He wondered if that made it more difficult to have the kind of lasting and authentic transaction Annette said she wanted her employees to recognize? Nathan decided to find out. He fingered the seven golden coins sitting in his jacket pocket.

When he got to the front of the line, the employee looked at Nathan waiting to be told what he wanted to order. Nathan fought back the urge to order the club sandwich he usually got.

"How's it going?" he said to the young man dutifully waiting.

"Okay," the young man answered. "It's been kinda busy today. What can I get you?"

"Well, what would you recommend? What's really good here?"

The young man seemed somewhat surprised by the question. "Uh, the mexi-chicken sub is good. It's kinda spicy. I like that."

"I'm not into spicy. How's the turkey, tomato and avocado wrap?"

The young man shrugged. "Sorry. Haven't tried it. I'm not really into avocados."

Another employee was assembling sandwiches to his right, but he didn't turn to ask her. He just shrugged again.

Nathan caved a bit. "Okay, I'll have the club."

"Sure," the young man said. "What kind of bread?" He seemed relieved not to have to engage in unscripted small talk, and deftly, though a little too methodically, assembled Nathan's sub. After he'd rung Nathan up and was handing him his receipt, he said, "Thanks for coming in. Have a good evening."

Nathan tried one more time. "Have a good evening yourself. And try the avocado wrap sometime, you might be surprised."

Reflexively, the young man responded," Sure." And quickly turned his attention to the next customer in line.

Nathan took his club sandwich out to his car. The young man had not taken the opportunity to engage with his customer, and Nathan had given him a couple prime openings. Could that be indicative of a minimum-wage attitude: *They don't pay me enough to make small talk. I'm not the owner, so what?*

Nathan didn't know. What he did realize was that he might not be sure what an authentic and lasting transaction felt like yet, but he sure knew what a meaningless exchange felt like.

And oddly, it made his club sandwich less satisfying. By the time he got to the nursing home, he couldn't even remember what the kid looked like.

Many assisted living facilities had the dubious distinction of being drab and colorless. That couldn't be said of the Aurora Community complex. It had gone from strictly vanilla to a 31-flavors color scheme. To Nathan it felt like every public space and hallway was a different bold color. He wondered if that was a strategy to help the residents navigate the place that ranged from independent-living apartments like his father's to 24-hour nursing care. Whatever the case, the vibrant, though cloying, colors led him easily to his father's room. Teal to red wine to sage green to burnt sienna got him there.

The good news was that his father was lucid. That meant he wouldn't be mixing up Nathan for Garrett. But it also meant they might butt heads. Ever since Nathan had passed on becoming a dentist, the eminent Dr. Danforth had questioned his decision making. And that had made for some rough encounters through the years. Which made the current situation so much harder for his dad to listen to his advice or accept his help.

Nathan learned from the on-duty nurse that his father had been the one to initiate help from the staff, complaining that he was hungry, but was having trouble swallowing. A speech pathologist had been assigned to evaluate his swallowing and was bringing him dinner at 6:00.

Nathan hoped that would shed some light on his father's condition. He took a seat across from his father in the compact kitchenette of his little apartment. Dr. Danforth Perkins had once been a tall man, over six feet, but he was now slightly hunched. His once-full face was now craggy and carved with the cares of eight decades. At times he looked lost and worn, though his green eyes could still pierce through the cloudy veil of age. Like they did now as he eyed his eldest son.

His father seemed to be sizing him up. He lifted his right hand and thrust his forefinger in his son's direction. "Where's Garrett?" he demanded.

"He and Beth took Marcy to her piano recital tonight."

"Why wasn't I told? I would go."

"Dad, you know Marcy gets nervous when lots of family show up to watch her. We didn't get invited either." Nathan's excuse was a half truth; the other half being that Danforth's health issues could make outings difficult.

His father dismissed the explanation with a wave of his hand. "Silly. The girl will get over it." He slapped his hand down on the table. "It's not like I have all the time in the world left. You should know that better than anyone, Nathan. You practically took half my life when you went to work at that window factory."

There it was. Less than a minute into his visit, an old wound reopened. As prepared for his father's criticism as he was, Nathan flinched nevertheless. "Sorry, Dad. But let's talk about something new. That's a lot of water under the ol' bridge."

"I still don't understand it."

"What's to understand? I didn't want to be a dentist."

"You never gave it a chance," his father pressed him. "Why would you want to work in a factory and run an assembly line when you could give real service to people. Be a professional. Be respected in your community."

Nathan's tempered flared for a moment. "Dad, I own a well respected company. I employ people. We produce quality products. I'm a small business owner just like you were!" He stared hard at his father, his glazed expression, and exhaled very slowly. He shrugged. "Okay, really, let's talk about something else. Lisa got a job in the mall last week. They build teddy bears for kids."

"Teddy bears?"

"Yeah, custom teddy bears. They assemble them right in the shop. I guess it's pretty popular."

"Sounds ridiculous. Why would Jillian want to make teddy bears? What's wrong with the flower shop? Did she get fired? Or did she have to take on another job because your windows aren't selling?"

It was always tricky when his father's memory became confused. Nathan fought the temptation to raise his voice. The problem couldn't be solved by talking louder; his father wasn't hard of hearing. He had to try to finesse the conversation and hope for the best.

"No, Dad. Everything's fine. Lisa, our daughter, is working at the teddy bear shop. Jillian is still at the flower shop. We're all okay."

His father's eye's suddenly dimmed as if a veil had dropped. "Your mother liked flowers. Alstroemeria. Those were her favorite. Would always make her happy. She liked taking you boys to the play park in the summer because out by the teeter-totters and swings, they had beds and beds of Alstroemeria. One time she lost track of you and finally found you in the flower beds picking alstroemeria for her. You always made her so happy."

Nathan became as lost in the moment as his father. It was the kind of seesaw they rode. One moment up and the next down. He wanted so much for his father to understand he was there for him.

Would always be. He felt moved go to him now. Give him a hug and show him the love he felt.

But there was a knock on the door.

Nathan quickly rose and opened the door. A woman stood holding a tray of food. "Hi. I'm Trish Coleman, I'm the staff speech pathologist. I've brought Mr. Perkins' dinner, if this is a good time."

"Absolutely," Nathan said. "Should I leave?"

"Not at all," Trish said. "Are you family?"

"I'm his son. I'm Nathan Perkins."

"Pleased to meet you Mr. Perkins," Trish said. Then she turned to Nathan's father, "And I'm pleased to meet you, Mr. Perkins. I'm here because you mentioned to the nurse you were having trouble swallowing." Her voice was warm and inviting.

Nathan's father nodded, pointing to his Adam's apple. "Things aren't going down so well. Keep coughing even when I'm just drinking water, so I haven't wanted to eat."

Trish set the tray on the table. "Well, Mr. Perkins, drinking water is trickier than most people think, especially if it's room temperature. There's no texture and without a temperature variation sometimes our swallowing reflexes aren't fully triggered. The most common mistake—and I'm as guilty as anyone—is tilting your head back to swallow. That just opens the airway and can lead to aspiration. I do it all the time and I should know better," she said with a quick laugh.

"Yeah, doctors don't like to take their own medicine," Danforth said. "I was a dentist for over forty years. Hated flossing. I only did it grudgingly."

"You never let us skip. And now it's hardwired," Nathan said.

"That's right and you've got healthy teeth and gums. Sometimes it's worth listening to your father, Nathan."

Trish noted the hard look that passed from father to son and took the initiative. "So, *Doctor* Perkins, you're a dentist. Excellent. I'm sure you've looked in more mouths than I probably ever will, and you'll know just what I'm talking about anatomically. You might even be able to teach me a thing or two."

Nathan's father turned to her looking pleased. "That I might. What's for dinner?"

Trish smiled and began to uncover the dishes on the tray explaining why she ordered the various foods and that Dr. Perkins could choose which ones he wanted to try. She'd observe him eating and make suggestions and take notes.

Her friendly manner and complete engagement with his father impressed Nathan. In no time at all she'd made a friend of him. He watched closely as she went about her job.

She chatted as his father ate. She suggested he chew each bite a bit more and tilt his chin down when swallowing. He did so. But when he took a drink of milk. He tilted his head back and began coughing. Milk shot from his mouth, and Nathan was on his feet. "Is he okay? Is he choking?"

Trish held her palm out to him calmly. "He's okay. You always want to watch for his breathing. See, he just took a quick breath. You only hit the panic button when he can't get a breath."

She moved around the table and put a hand on his father's shoulder until his coughing stopped. "It's like we were talking about earlier, Dr. Perkins. When you tilt your head back, you open the airway. I think that's what's happening."

"Didn't used to be that way." Nathan's father's voice was gruff, but not his manner,

Trish sighed and smiled. "Yeah, we can all say that about a lot of things. I certainly didn't used to have wrinkles, grey hairs or mysterious pounds accumulating. But, even we old dogs can learn a few tricks to compensate."

"You're a young pup. I'm the old dog here," he growled.

"You still got some bite," Trish bantered. "Now, you ready to try that drink again? Tilt your chin down, take a sip and swallow—but don't raise your chin."

Nathan's father dipped his head and tilted the glass of milk to his lips. He stopped. "Feels awkward," he grumbled.

"Yes," Trish agreed. "It is, but it's safer."

After another false start he took a swallow. He didn't cough. He took another and swallowed fine, though self consciously.

He set his glass down. "Seemed to work."

"Always glad when my advice does the trick," Trish said. "But you'll want to take it slow. I'll stay until you're finished with dinner."

Trish proceeded to make light conversation as Nathan's father ate his meal and finished his milk. He had no other problems and seemed to enjoy Trish asking about his dental practice and oral health. When he was finished eating, she placed her business card on the table near him.

"You be sure to call if you have any other swallowing problems. Don't hesitate. I want you eating, drinking and staying healthy."

Nathan's father nodded. "Thanks, Miss."

"My pleasure, Dr. Perkins. We're here for you."

The way she said it made Nathan believe she really meant it. Trish shook his father's hand and picked up the almost-empty tray. Nathan opened the door for her.

"Thanks," Trish acknowledged.

"Thank *you*," Nathan responded. He held out his hand and Trish shook it. "We really appreciate your help."

"At your service," Trish said with a smile and headed down the hall.

"Nice gal," Danforth said when Nathan sat back down. "Knows her stuff."

"Good bedside manner, too," Nathan added.

His father nodded. "Treat people right. Like you'd treat family."

Nathan smiled at the irony of that since his father had not always treated him in a family friendly way. That was the other side of family. There could be bad blood. Deep memories. Deep hurts. Still, Nathan was struck by what his father was saying in regards to Trish.

"You're right," he told him. "Hang on a second, Dad. I'll be right back."

Nathan went out the door and jogged in the direction Trish had gone. He caught up with her near the dining hall. "Excuse me, Ms. Coleman."

Trish turned around. "Mr. Perkins. Is anything the matter? Does your father need help?"

"No, no," Nathan answered as he reached into his pocket. "I just want to thank you again. And," he hesitated, "this may seem silly, but I'd like to give you this."

He held out one of Annette's golden coins. "A small business owner challenged me to recognize good service when I saw it. She had these coins made. It's literally a token of a job well done. You really made a positive impression on my dad, which is not always an easy thing to do."

Trish took the coin from him and looked at it. "Now, this doesn't happen to me everyday."

"It probably should. You're great at your job," Nathan complimented.

She waved his compliment away. "I'm lucky. I enjoy working with people—especially someone like your father who has so much life experience. I appreciate the thought behind the coin. It'll be a nice memento."

"I'll let you get back to your rounds. Thanks again," Nathan said and started back to his father's room. He felt so upbeat, he almost started whistling. Something he couldn't remember having done for months.

A meaningful transaction.

He recognized how both his father and Trish had benefited from their interaction. His father had received important swallowing advice and been given a nice measure of respect by Trish. On her part, Trish had the satisfaction of helping a patient and talking shop with his father.

Trish had done more than her job, she'd reached out and genuinely connected with her father. Nathan was glad he'd followed through with Annette's challenge by giving Trish the coin. Maybe there was something to her way of approaching business.

The nicest part was that Nathan didn't dread going back in his father's room. Maybe they wouldn't have a whole lot to say the rest of his stay, but Nathan would stay positive. He'd give it his best and be there for his father. That's really all he ever had to do, and he wondered why it seemed so hard these days.

"Coffee?" Garrett asked Tuesday morning as Nathan looked through the documents their father's attorney had dropped off. Garrett was already in his white lab jacket looking every bit the dentist. In fact, Nathan had to admit that his younger brother in many ways had become the second coming of Dr. Danville Perkins. He'd become a linchpin in the local dental community and had very loyal patients. To Nathan, he seemed to be on cruise control.

"Sure," Nathan replied to his brother's offer. He set down the papers he'd been scanning. "So, Dad's made you his executor? That's not surprising, since he already gave you power of attorney."

Garrett looked up from pouring the coffee. "I wanted to make sure you knew about it. You know I feel strange that he puts this all in my hands. You're the eldest."

"Yeah, but you became the dentist."

"I wish he'd get over that. Such a waste of energy."

"I'm sure my attitude had something to do with it, too," Nathan admitted. "When I was younger, I wasn't very apologetic. Dad must've thought he was handing me the world—champagne and caviar—and his ungrateful son chose beer and pretzels. To him, I'm sure I sounded pretty unreasonable, maybe ungrateful. To him, Winning Windows is just a factory job—not a real profession like dentistry."

"Did you two argue last night?" Garrett asked.

"He got to me for a moment, but then I realized that he isn't himself. He's living in a past—maybe I am too—but I can't let us drift farther apart. I've got to find some middle ground with him and be positive. I know he must feel lost. That's got to be tough, like you said yesterday."

"Yeah. It's tough on him. Tough on all of us," Garrett observed, handing Nathan his coffee.

"There's not much I can do about how Dad feels, except support him. I don't want this part of his life to be harsh and bitter. I can't control his attitude, but I hate to see him sour on everything and everyone. That's not how he lived and I don't want him going that way to his grave."

"Did he look bad last night?" Garrett asked.

"At first he did. But the speech pathologist really helped with his swallowing, and Dad ate a substantial dinner. It really perked him up, and afterwards he was in better sprits than I've seen him in a long time. We actually had a decent visit. He reminisced about the Orchard."

Nathan leaned back in his chair. "I haven't heard him talk about his childhood like that in a decade. He was almost wistful, going on about working the farm and picking apples."

"He loved the Orchard. I think it's his Rosebud, if you know what I mean," Garrett confided. "Being the farm boy, milking the cows and climbing those apple trees. It's easy to romanticize those things now, but I'm sure it was a ton of work for him. All those 'carefree' chores before he got shoveled off to dental school to become respectable and elevate the family name."

Nathan nodded in understanding. "Yeah, Dad worked his tail off to get that *Dr.* in front of his name, just like Grandpa and Grandma Perkins always dreamed. They were so proud of him. Just like Dad and Mom were proud of you when you got your dental degree."

Garrett shook away his brother's compliment. "They were proud of us both," he said, quickly changing the subject. "How was his memory? Did he mix us up at all?"

"He was pretty lucid, especially after dinner. When I first got there and was talking to him, he did confuse Lisa with Jillian when I tried to tell him about Lisa's job at the mall. He wanted to know why Jillian suddenly wanted to make teddy bears rather than floral arrangements."

Garrett grinned knowingly.

"You know how it is." Nathan leaned towards his brother smiling. "Speaking of amusing, Jillian told me a story last night about work. Yesterday morning, a customer came in to her department wanting to return an arrangement of cut flowers that was two days old because they were wilting. She got testy about the store's claim of using 'only the freshest flowers.'"

Garrett's eyes rolled. "What'd Jillian do?"

"Jillian remembered the woman because she'd sold her the flowers which came with a promotional vase. The woman had even asked Jillian to re-arrange the flowers in the vase before leaving the store. When Jillian looked at the wilting flowers in the vase the woman was returning, there was no hint that the customer had ever put water in it. The vase and the flowers were bone dry."

Nathan smiled sardonically before continuing. "So, Jillian asked the woman if she'd put water in the vase when she'd gotten home. The woman became indignant and said that wasn't her fault. That Jillian should've put water in the vase before she left the store."

"I hope Jillian didn't punch her."

"No, Jillian is Jillian. She put new flowers in the vase, filled it with water and apologized for the inconvenience."

Garrett laughed. "So, what's Jillian going to do when the woman comes back in demanding that she clean up the mess in her car after the vase spills on her way home?"

"Then she might punch her." Nathan joined the laughter of his brother.

Garrett shook his head. "I've had my share of crazy patients. I'm sure you have too. Hard to know what makes them tick."

"Oh, I don't know. Those kind of people are generally one-dimensional," Nathan tried to explain. "It's always about them. Completely self centered. No give and take. All blame, no responsibility."

Something clicked for Nathan when he heard himself say the *all blame, no responsibility* line. It seemed to focus on a key element of a meaningful transaction. Both sides had to be invested in the interaction. Both had to be responsible for a satisfactory outcome. Both parties had to put themselves on the line in some way. You had to risk something—something you valued (money, things, self respect, love, happiness, etc.)—for an authentic exchange to take place.

Failure or rejection always had to be a part of the equation. If you didn't care about the outcome, didn't believe you were responsible in some way, it was just a one-sided exchange. Nathan could see how Jillian had put herself out there to resolve the case of the waterless vase, but the customer had wrapped herself in indignant self armor and worked her way into a ridiculous corner.

Nathan also saw that he had ventured a little ways out on a limb with the employee at the sub sandwich shop, but the kid had ignored the opportunity. Only Trish, the speech pathologist, had been able to establish the sense of trust with Nathan's father. A sense that they were in the situation together. That had been the basis for their successful interaction.

It wasn't rocket science, though there was Newtonian logic. An equal and opposite reaction. Both sides giving and taking, granting and receiving, promising and delivering.

Nathan's epiphany was interrupted by Garrett. "Jillian's customer sounds like a doozy. Dad told me when I started here with him that you should only give up on patients when they've lost respect for themselves. He used to say, 'There's no value when there are no values.' He sure had that right."

Gesturing to the documents Nathan had been looking through, he continued, "And that's why I wanted you to look over the documents before I sign and return them to Dad's lawyer. We have to be open and equal about this. We are in this together, even if Dad doesn't always see it that way."

"Thanks, Garrett," Nathan acknowledged. "I'd never mistrust you or your judgment, but I appreciate you keeping me in the loop." He stood up and shook his brother's hand. For an instant he considered giving

Garrett one of Annette's golden coins, but he wondered if that would somehow cheapen this transaction. It didn't feel quite right with family. This wasn't business. This was blood.

"Well, I'm glad Dad seems to be doing better," Garrett said. "I'll visit him this evening and tell him about Marcy's recital."

"He'll be glad to hear about it, though he told me that he wanted to go."

Garrett smiled. "Taking him places is always tricky."

"You don't have to convince me," agreed Nathan. "Let's talk tomorrow and maybe we can arrange an outing for Dad this weekend. It'd be good for him."

Good for me, too, Nathan thought. He'd actually enjoyed listening to his father last night. As long as the topic was the distant past, they seemed to be on safe ground. His father had always appreciated an attentive audience, and Nathan was content to be it last night.

He left Garrett's dental practice for Winning Windows feeling pretty good. In talking with his brother, Nathan had gained a firmer grasp of the source of a meaningful transaction and what it should feel like. Though, he was still uncertain how the concept translated into his everyday world of business. Service industries like health care were one thing. Selling composite windows was another.

Wasn't it?

On the way to his office, he resisted once again the temptation to stop at Seven Coins for a cup of coffee and a splash of Annette's advice.

Nathan wondered if he had begun to obsess over Annette's transaction coins. It was late Tuesday afternoon. His day had gone pretty well. In fact, things were looking good for the Sunset Gardens apartment complex contract. He'd spoken to Mike Corbin, one of the lead contractors on the 180 unit project. Mike had explained that the bids put in by Winning Windows and AMVIC Windows were the only two being considered. That was encouraging news, though Nathan knew AMVIC's up-front price would be lower. It was always lower.

Nathan thought about how Annette's coffee shop was going up against Starbucks and couldn't possibly compete on price. It was the same with AMVIC, which didn't have the clout of the big green mermaid, but was many times the size of Winning Windows.

If Gracie and Estevan were able to snag the Sunset Gardens contract, it would be a big boost for Winning Windows. Nathan would be able to bring back a few of his part time employees to complete the order. Considering that possibility made him feel good.

What made him feel uncomfortable was that Estevan and Gracie couldn't agree on how to negotiate the contract. Gracie thought they should spend their time getting a slew of customer testimonials together. While Estevan wanted to spend their time producing documentation on the green angle of their product. In addition to the great energy savings, they could convince the contractor to tout the fact that his materials were produced locally, making the overall carbon footprint of the apartment complex much smaller.

It was times like this that Nathan missed having a sales manager. Gracie and Estevan were energetic and earnest, but he sometimes wondered if they really saw the company like he did. It'd been a while since he'd been active on the sales end, and he wondered why his sales team couldn't just sell their windows on the quality and value of their manufacture. Nathan knew they made top notch triple-paned windows. Gracie and Estevan knew that as well. Why couldn't they communicate that without all the rigmarole and hard-sell games?

He thought about the six remaining coins. The Sunset Gardens transaction was huge. How could he translate the idea behind those simple metal coins into something meaningful for his business? He'd given one coin away to Trish, the speech pathologist at

Aurora Community. Would he be able to give the other coins away by Monday? Would any be to Gracie or Estevan or any of his employees?

His cell phone rang. The ringtone was "It's a Small World." His daughter, Lisa, had chosen it for him because she said she wanted him to remember that it's a small, small *business* world, and that people like him all around the globe made people happy. Nathan liked the sentiment.

"Hey, sweetie, what's up?" he answered.

"Hi, Dad, how's your day been?"

"Good," he said. "Yours?"

"School was fine, but I have a little problem. I've got work in about an hour and the tire on the Honda went flat again."

"The same one?"

"Yeah."

"Okay. I can be home in about twenty minutes."

"Thanks, Dad. Sorry for the hassle."

"No worries. See you in a few." Nathan ended the call. He told Gracie and Estevan he had to leave, but if they had any questions about the Sunset Gardens bid to call on his cell.

As he drove home, he became more and more irritated about the flat tire. The past Saturday he'd taken the tire to get fixed because it had developed a slow leak. The tire shop was a place he'd gone to for years. It was clean, fast and efficient. He'd always gotten good service there, so he wondered what had happened. In this economy, you never quite knew. Businesses that had been around for a long time had lost their bearing—or their competitive edge—and folded.

He knew that's what was worrying him about Winning Windows. Could his company be slowly fading out? Was he part of the problem? Had he fallen asleep at the helm? Nathan battled those nagging questions all the way home.

When he arrived, Nathan put the spare on Lisa's Civic. It went quickly, since he'd changed the exact same tire three days earlier.

His daughter was gushing with gratitude. "Thanks, Daddy. You're the best. The spare will get me to work, and then I can take the flat in to get fixed tomorrow afternoon, so you won't have to deal with it."

"Oh, I want to deal with this," Nathan said, his voice stern. "This wasn't your fault, Lisa. I want to see what those bozos at the tire shop did. You take my car to work. I'm gonna run this over to the tire shop right now and find out what happened. I don't like the thought that this could've stranded you somewhere late at night."

"Okay. Just don't blow a gasket." Lisa warned, though she knew better than to get in her dad's way when he'd gathered a full head of steam.

Nathan frowned for a moment, and then chuckled. "Where'd you learn that phrase?"

"Hey, I am in Honors English. I read a lot."

"Right. Well, have a good shift building bears. Make the kids happy."

"The kids are easy. It's the parents who make all the demands. Your generation is so tough to please." She gave him a quick hug, grabbed her purse and headed out the door.

Nathan stood there with a dumb smile on his face. He'd just changed a flat tire and, in payment, received a sarcastic remark and a hug from his daughter. Yet, he felt as if he'd gotten the better part of the bargain. That was not in any business class he'd taken or marketing book he'd read. As he went to the sink to clean up, he wondered why that was.

The shop was a cacophony of impact wrenches and guys yelling back and forth. Nathan had always liked the service here. No matter how busy it was, within a few seconds of pulling in, one of the employees was hustling up to your car. The shop tried to upsell on every purchase, but they weren't pushy about it. Nathan understood.

They were a business like his and wanted to make a profit. He always gave Gracie and Estevan his blessing to upsell as well, as long as they listened to what their customers really wanted and what they could afford. You didn't have to be pushy to get customers to recognize quality products and service. You just had to take the time to find out what they really needed.

A young man with *Steve* on his nametag greeted him and Nathan explained what had happened and opened the Civic's trunk to get at the flat tire in it. He also handed Steve the receipt for the tire repair done the previous Saturday. Before he had a chance to get irate about it, Steve pre-empted him by grabbing the flat tire out of the trunk.

"Sorry about that, Mr. Perkins," the young man apologized, after he looked at the receipt. "I'll check out what happened with the tire. It might take a half hour or so. I've got a few people in front of you, but I think we can get you taken care of this evening if you're willing to wait a bit."

"Sure, if it won't be too long," Nathan assented.

"Great," Steve said, "Why don't you go inside and have a seat. I'll get to this as soon as I can."

The young man's earnestness was convincing, and Nathan went into the clean, well-lighted waiting area. Almost every seat was full, so Nathan stood by a large window. It was an older aluminum cased double paned job. Looking around, Nathan figured that with all the glass in the waiting area, the shop owner could cut their thermal loss by a third if they replaced the older windows with his commercial triple-paned windows. It'd mean substantial energy savings for the shop.

New windows would be a great investment for a place like this—and a lot of others, but it's not always easy convincing folks to put out ten thousand dollars now in order to save twenty thousand over the next decade. It took time and trust.

Twenty-five minutes later, ten minutes after the shop officially closed. Steve approached Nathan who was reading a newspaper.

"Mr. Perkins, I'm all done. Either you got another metal fragment in the last couple of days, or we missed a piece deep in the tread. Either way I think we got it fixed for real this time. Let's get you checked out."

Nathan followed the young man to the counter to a middle-aged man whose name badge identified him as Chuck, the manager. He took the paperwork from Steve and looked it over. Then he smiled at Nathan and began to say, "That's $25..."

Before he could finish, Nathan interrupted. "Hold on. I don't think I should have to pay anything, since it doesn't appear you fixed the tire on Saturday." He glared fixedly at the Chuck.

Chuck smiled back. "Exactly, Mr. Perkins. You don't owe us anything. The $25 is a credit towards any future purchase or service at the shop. We stand by our work and when we miss something or make a mistake we credit the customer for the inconvenience."

Nonplussed, Nathan looked from Chuck to Steve. "Really?" he almost stammered.

"We know your time is valuable," Chuck said.

"I'm impressed," Nathan admitted. "I was ready for a fight."

"We try to avoid those here. We've got enough to keep us busy, so please accept our voucher and have a good evening." Chuck handed Nathan the paper-work with the credit voucher on it.

Nathan took the paperwork and looked at the voucher. He fished into his jacket pocket and brought out one of Annette's coins. "Well, then, please accept this from me. It's a token of good service. A fellow small business owner is trying to convince me that there are folks who still understand a good transaction," Nathan explained.

Chuck took the coin and examined the handshake on it. "Old school. I like that." He handed it to Steve, so he could have a look. "So, what's your business?" Chuck asked.

Nathan took out his business card. "Winning Windows. We're over near Canyon Park, close to Thrasher's Corner."

Chuck nodded. "That makes sense. I noticed you examining our windows as you were waiting."

"Just a habit," Nathan confessed.

"You think we're due for an upgrade?" Chuck asked.

Nathan hemmed for a moment. "Probably wouldn't hurt. These look thirty years old."

Chuck grinned. "At least." He looked at Nathan's business card. "Well, Mr. Perkins, now I know someone to call if I think about replacing them."

"Sure. I'd be happy to answer any questions you might have."

"Will do," Chuck said, extending his hand.

Nathan shook it.

"I don't know if I really need a coin to remind me how to do good business, but I like the sentiment behind it," Chuck said, motioning to Steve. "I'll let him keep it. You have a fine evening now, Mr. Perkins."

"I will. You, too," Nathan said, giving a brief wave to Chuck and then Steve. It was only then that he noticed the family resemblance between the two.

Father and son? They could be. Nathan considered how easy it was to pass on your genes without ever having to think about it. Your values? That was a whole different story. Passing on your hard earned values took a lot more time, commitment and work.

As he drove home, all repaired and revved up, Nathan found himself whistling "It's a Small World."

The dream again. The dusty road. The sense of urgency. Dusk falling. Night coming. Where to go for safety?

Nathan woke. His arm was numb, tucked awkwardly under his chest. He cautiously rolled off it, feeling the emergence of tiny pins pricking his forearm as blood began to recirculate. The dream wasn't all that mysterious, wasn't all that complicated, so why did he keep having it?

I know I'm in trouble. I'm looking for answers. Leave me be!

So many things could be lost by not paying attention, by letting them slowly drift away. That drift had caused him to lose his relationship with his father. And he feared it would be the same with his business.

Things just don't just drift away. You have to allow it. Nathan, if you can 'be' scared, you can just as easily 'be' brave. So come on already. Be something!

Nathan sighed quietly. Being human was complicated. So much you wanted to control, but so little you really could. Nathan couldn't control his father's attitude towards him or the Sunset Gardens contract. He couldn't command any of those things. He bunched his pillow under his head and breathed slowly. He didn't even have power over his own dreams which continued to torment him.

He knew he needed to be more intentional about his family and his work. Rolling back on his side, Nathan closed his eyes. So much good to consider. That's what was important. What was of value to himself. He couldn't keep second guessing his decisions. If they were based on what was truly important, loving his family and friends and serving his clients well, then it would all work out. He vowed to find the way, the road would be clear.

Nathan slept peacefully the rest of the night.

As he worked on his company's quarterly report late Wednesday morning, Nathan was wishing he 'needed' more of Annette's golden coins. When he'd stopped by Seven Coins Coffee on the way into work Annette had seemed surprised when he told her he'd given away two of the golden transaction coins. *That's great. When you have time I want to hear about these transactions and your reaction*, she'd said.

The shop had been busy, and Annette was working the register, so Nathan promised he'd try to stop by in the next couple days to catch her up. "Maybe I should give you a few more coins," Annette had offered, but Nathan declined, explaining to her that he was already feeling enough pressure to give away his five remaining tokens.

Now he was wishing he had reason to give some of those coins to his employees. Gracie and Estevan were still quibbling over Sunset Gardens. In the assembly area he'd found Foster chewing out a fellow worker for mixing up some measurements. Not the kind of *golden* transactions he was hoping he'd see in his company.

His phone rang. It was Garrett.

"What's up?" Nathan asked his brother.

"I went over to Dad's last night."

"How was he doing?"

"Well, good. Spooky good, actually. I haven't seen him this animated in almost a year," Garrett said. "And when I mentioned the possibility of an outing this weekend, he said he wanted to see the Orchard."

"Really?"

"Yeah. He was adamant. What do you think?"

Nathan considered the question for a moment. "When I saw him Monday, he was doing some heavy reminiscing about the place. I guess he's kind of fixated on it. I don't see a big problem with it. Are you free this Saturday?"

"I am and so is Beth. We can take him."

"Jillian and I will come, too. We'll be the back up," Nathan suggested.

"Always a good thing when taking Dad somewhere these days." Garrett paused. "I kinda think it could be fun. Dad was so jazzed talking about the Orchard last night."

"It's where he grew up. Those roots run deep. I hope he won't be disappointed or become disoriented. The place is a lot more commercial these days."

"Yeah, but the apple groves haven't changed much or the outbuildings. We'll just keep him away from the market and gift shop."

"True enough. Hey, if you want to run by Dad's tonight and tell him, I think he'd appreciate you wanting to come too."

Nathan paused. "I don't know. I might be pressing my luck. We had a decent visit last time. I don't want to jinx it."

"Honestly," Garrett said, "I think he may be mellowing."

"That's hopeful, but I'm not holding my breath."

"I thought you were trying to be more optimistic," Garrett chided.

"Well, I'm trying, but I've got the same stubborn streak as Dad," Nathan admitted.

"Exactly. That's why you're living your own life and I'm just the sequel to Dr. Danforth's."

"Am I hearing some regret, little brother?"

"Naaaaw," Garrett drawled. "I like being a dentist, but it was the path of least resistance for me. I'm just lucky it was one I'm well suited for."

"Okay, then. I'll drop by Dad's this evening and spring the plan," Nathan promised. "Then we'll talk and make the arrangements for Saturday."

"Sounds good. Let's touch base tomorrow."

After hanging up, Nathan leaned back in his office chair and closed his eyes. He imagined his father as a young boy climbing the apple trees in the Orchard, shaking the limbs and watching those red delicious apples bounce on their stems. Did his dad dream about his youth? Trying to relive his own life in some vivid and mysterious way?

He'd known his father for over half a century and he felt he understood very little about what made him tick. And then it struck him that his father might feel much the same way about his son. Maybe, at night, his dad was dreaming along that same dusty road, looking to find Nathan.

Nathan's brief "ah-ha" was interrupted by the phone. He checked the caller ID number before picking it up. It was *unknown*.

"Winning Windows," he answered, "Nathan Perkins speaking."

"Hi Nathan, this is Annette Florence from Seven Coins Coffee."

Nathan was surprised. "Hi, Annette, I didn't expect to hear from you so soon. You looked pretty slammed earlier this morning."

"Well, I had a little break and looked up Winning Windows website for your number. I thought I'd take a chance and call to see if you have a minute to talk."

"Sure. The web certainly makes it easier to get connected."

"It does," Annette agreed, "though face to face is the best—and talking on the phone is probably the next best thing."

"What no Facebook and Twitter?" Nathan asked with a hint of sarcasm.

Annette laughed. "Oh, they have their place, you know. I feel like I can follow what my friends and family are up to a bit better. Yet, it doesn't make me feel like I know them that much better. To feel more connected I need a real chat."

"I hear you on that," Nathan said. "The virtual world is amazing, but it ain't everything."

"Absolutely. I think both old and new approaches have their place in getting folks together. I put up a bulletin board here at the shop and half of it is already covered in business cards. I've come to believe that people like the opportunity to make connections — no matter what the medium. My thinking on the bulletin board is if you're like-minded enough to come into Seven Coins, you would probably rather do business with someone who shares your appreciation for this place or, at least, your taste in coffee. You know, we're building a bit of a tribe here."

"You're right about that," Nathan said, thinking about the business card he'd given to Chuck, the manager at the tire shop last night. "Finding common ground is the best way to get your business foot in the door."

"Exactly," Annette agreed. "And on that note, I was hoping to follow up on what you told me this morning about the transaction coins. It helps a lot if I can share these stories when I meet with my employees. Makes them see that my ideas around service are not completely crazy. Especially, if a fellow business owner is seeing some value in doing the same thing."

"So far, I'd say you aren't crazy, though the two people I've given them to might have thought I was," Nathan added with a laugh. "They were two very different kinds of transactions."

"Great. Do you have time to tell me about them?"

"Sure." He prefaced his account by telling Annette about his father and how he'd gone to visit him Monday night. Nathan told her about stopping at the sandwich shop and being disappointed with the almost mechanized service there. Then he related the story of Trish, the speech pathologist, who'd evaluated his father's swallowing. How she provided him with a warm and personalized approach that really worked with his father. He finished with his account of the tire shop's policy of standing behind their work and crediting him for the time to re-repair his daughter's flat tire.

"So how'd you know these were authentic transactions?" Annette asked when he was through.

"Because I felt great after them. I felt like I'd gotten everything I could've expected and I was uplifted."

"Okay, what about the people you gave the coins to? What do you think they got out of the deal? Remember in a good transaction, both parties benefit."

Nathan paused, collecting his thoughts. "The speech pathologist seemed to enjoy the back and forth with my father. He was a dentist, so they talked a bit about the connection between oral health and overall health. They had some common ground. She just seemed to be a person who enjoys people, and her advice to my father had an immediate and positive effect. I'd think that would be very satisfying for her."

"I agree," Annette said. "It's the difference between doing a job and doing what you love to do. Fortunate are the people who love their job. Amazing are the employees who don't necessarily love their jobs, but would never let the customer see that. Most people get a lot of satisfaction from helping others. Why else would people volunteer?

"I think your analysis of what the speech pathologist got out of the transaction is solid. She connected with your father and helped him. So, how about your father? Did you see that he got something out of the interaction?"

"Hmmm, I hadn't thought about it, Annette. But you know, Dad and I had a very easy visit after she left. I was in better spirits after giving the speech pathologist the coin, and I think Dad enjoyed her attention and the banter about something he devoted most of his life to: oral health. I think I've discounted the true impact this 'transaction' had on everyone in the room."

"Nice observation, Nathan. In the same way you may walk out of Seven Coins with a bounce in your step because it was a good experience, your Dad and the speech pathologist shared a positive interaction and it spilled over into the entire evening for you.

"Now, what about the guys at the tire shop?" Annette asked. "Seems to me they lost money on your transaction."

"That one I'm a bit unsure of. Maybe they got a kick out of my look of shock when I was ready to argue over having to pay to re-fix the tire and instead they gave me a credit." Drumming his fingers on his desk, Nathan tried to put himself back in the moment of the tire shop last night. "Maybe in the short term they lost money. I didn't pay them for any of the time they spent repairing the tire and they gave me a credit for future work. But I'll bet they're banking I'll be back because I got such good service. And, they're right. I've always liked the place and now I have even more reason to return."

Annette summed it up. "So, you got the tire fixed and a credit, not to mention a sense that they respected and valued your time. And they solidified your customer loyalty and repeat business—and maybe some word-of-mouth referrals because you'll be telling that story to other folks. It sure seems like both sides got something they each value and that it was pretty evenly balanced, which makes it a meaningful transaction."

"Yeah, I can see the importance of considering both sides of the interaction. If it's just one side feeling good after the experience, it can't be an authentic transaction, huh?"

"Not necessarily," Annette warned. "The exchange has to be balanced. And it might not always leave people happy. Not all meaningful transactions leave both parties smiling. In fact they could leave you crying—or raging. Sometimes in a transaction we get something we need and ultimately value—though we may not recognize it at the time—and it feels negative. It feels like we lost something."

"You mean, like an argument?" Nathan asked.

"Could be," Annette answered. "Think about a time when someone told you something you didn't want to hear, but it was the truth. You might have been angry or hurt. That's what you initially felt, but over time you realized the point of it and possibly came to appreciate the person for telling it to you straight. In the balance, the person who told you the truth feels the satisfaction of having helped you, and you gain from recognizing something about yourself. Plus you both share a deeper sense of trust. Transactions are at the core of all human relationships—this is not just a business thing. Remember, I got this insight from a preacher in Walla Walla. He wasn't trying to sell anything, except the Golden Rule."

"As always, Annette, you've given me another drink from the fire hose," Nathan remarked with a laugh. "I'm glad you called."

"It's worked out well for both of us. I've got your stories to share with my staff tomorrow, and you may have a better sense of how you might be able to give out those five coins you have left."

"Sounds like we just had a meaningful transaction. Even though I tried the other day, you sure I can't give you one of these coins?"

Annette laughed. "No. I've got plenty of my own. I appreciate the offer though, and I'm glad to be of help. Just keep your eyes, mind and heart open. You're beginning to see more clearly."

"Well, for a window manufacturer, that's always a good thing. Thanks for calling."

"You bet. Take care now."

Nathan hung up, sat back in his chair and closed his eyes, feeling as positive about his business as he had in a long while. It felt good to have some confidence back.

But his confidence was quickly shaken.

"I got in an argument with Gracie and Estevan," Nathan confessed under the steady eye of Foster at his assembly table. Patiently, Foster waited for the details, but Nathan wasn't sure he wanted to provide them. He hadn't so much argued as vented.

Why couldn't they work together better? Why'd they always have to be sniping at each other and their ideas? Nathan told them it was counterproductive and costing them customers, though he didn't really know if that was the case.

Gracie and Estevan had looked blindsided by his criticisms and Gracie retreated into their office and closed the door. Estevan had looked helplessly after her and Nathan immediately began to backtrack saying he was sorry, using the excuse that he was feeling a lot of pressure about the Sunset Gardens apartment complex contract to boost morale and their bottom line.

Nathan could have told Foster all of that, but then he'd have to tell him the underlying motivation. It was a clumsy attempt to force a meaningful transaction on Gracie and Estevan. When he'd spoken to Annette on the phone, she'd cautioned him that not all transactions were feel-good events. Nathan had thought by confronting Gracie and Estevan that he'd wake them up and make them change their style of interacting.

But, as Foster calmly waited him out, Nathan knew he'd only mugged Gracie and Estevan. He'd bullied and attacked them with his version of the truth. The boss's version. He hadn't engaged them in real problem solving. He'd unreasonably demanded vague and undefined change: get better and get better fast.

That could sound good, but he'd given them no direction. No game plan. Honestly, he didn't know what to do any better than Gracie or Estevan. He just had some gold coins and a gut feeling that Annette was onto something. The hard part was translating that into something meaningful for his employees. He was hoping Foster, who'd been with the company even longer than he had, could give him some perspective. Or maybe even bail him out of the mess he'd made.

"Okay, it wasn't really an argument," Nathan finally admitted to Foster. "It was a threat. We need this Sunset Gardens work, and I'm not sure how we're going to seal the deal with the two of them bickering. I'm stuck. I need Gracie and Estevan to be a team working with me, but I think I just alienated them instead."

Nathan shook his head dejectedly. "I even told Gracie she needs to watch how she sometimes rolls her eyes at customers. Bad move. Bad boss."

Foster rolled a toothpick from left to right in his mouth. "Bad boss. No doubt. I thought you were going to stop worrying so much."

"It's obvious I can't," Nathan acknowledged. "Too much on my mind."

"Then share the load," Foster suggested. "Lotsa folks here can help."

Nathan smiled. "Sounds so easy when you say it. But how?"

"No clue." Foster rolled the toothpick from right to left. "But, I'd start by asking Gracie and Estevan. They're the ones you most need as partners for Sunset Gardens."

"Yeah, but they probably despise me right now and think I'm blaming them for all of the company's problems."

Foster right eyebrow shot up. "So why are you standing here apologizing to *me*?"

"I'm explaining to you what happened."

"No. You're *apologizing to me* for accusing them. And they ain't here. Where's the sense in that, Nathan?" Foster challenged, his voice soft, precise and inescapable.

Nathan looked down at the window pieces Foster had spread out on his worktable. A puzzle that needed putting together, one piece at a time. "You're right. I need to be talking to Gracie and Estevan, not stalling out here. Thanks for the advice."

Nathan turned to go and then spun around to face Foster again. "Would you ever consider my job if I offered it to you?"

Foster didn't hesitate. "Sure. Most folks would like a shot at running a business. I'm no different, but you'd be foolish to hand the reins to me. I'd run this company, but I'd run it into the ground faster than a locomotive. I know how to make great windows, but I don't know half of what it takes to run a business."

"But you know people," Nathan pressed.

"Some. Especially myself. That's why I keep telling you I don't think automation is going to get us more business. I'd rely too much on the machines to do the right thing and not myself.

"See, Nathan. I've got to produce. Got to have a reason to matter. I put some of myself into each of these windows and some folks out there will notice that when they're looking out at the big, wide world."

He paused and rolled his toothpick back and forth. "I honestly don't know how you get other people to think like I do about producing quality. That's why you're the boss." Foster made a shooing motion. "Now, git. You've got a business to run, and I've got a window to build. You've just thrown off my productivity."

Nathan grinned. "Well, you probably just increased mine. Thanks."

Watching Nathan head to his office, Foster ritually rolled his toothpick a few times and then got back to the puzzle pieces that would become a winning window.

His father was watching the news when Nathan arrived at his Aurora Community apartment. *Watching* might not have been an accurate description. His father was staring at the screen, but he didn't seem to be seeing it. His eyes weren't glazed, as if he were under sedation; it was more like he was far away in his mind, seeing something from his memories.

It took a few moments of Nathan saying "Hi, Dad" before his father acknowledged him by pressing the mute button of the television remote on his armrest.

"Nathan?"

"Yes. It's me. How are you tonight, Dad?"

"Is Garrett coming?"

"No, I came tonight."

"I wanted to talk to Garrett. I want to go to the Orchard."

"He told me. We want to take you there on Saturday."

"What's today?"

"It's Wednesday, Dad. We'll come get you Saturday morning around ten, if that's okay."

A frown creased his father's already heavily creased forehead. "Why do you want to go to the Orchard?"

Nathan avoided sighing. He kept his voice bright and upbeat. "Because it'll be good to see the place again. I haven't been there in years. Jillian is going too."

His father drew back horrified. "What are you saying? Your mother is dead."

"No, Dad," Nathan reassured him. "Jillian is my wife. She is going to go with us."

"I thought you said *Gloria*," his father murmured. "God bless her."

Nathan nodded. Their conversation was on tenuous ground. Any mention of his mother could spin his father into a dark funk. Nathan tried to steer the conversation back on a safer footing.

"The weather is supposed to be clear this weekend, so the Orchard should be beautiful. Brisk, but beautiful," Nathan reiterated.

"What month is it?" his father asked.

"October. It'll be Halloween soon."

Dr. Danforth half smiled at some recollection. "They'll be burning leaves. I loved that smell."

Nathan didn't know if they still burned the leaves or composted them at the Orchard. "I remember that smell too when you'd take us out to see Grandpa and Grandma Perkins every fall. No place smelled more like autumn than the Orchard."

Dr. Danforth nodded. "Shame it got sold. I shouldn't have let them do it. A stupid mistake. My fault."

Nathan had never heard his father talk like that about his grandparents selling their land. That it was his fault. His father had only ever complained that they shouldn't have sold when they did, though Nathan knew they were lucky to have sold it to someone who'd kept it as a working farm. The beauty of the place had been saved, though commercialized. Farming and tourism had become strange bedfellows these days.

Deciding that a change of subject might be best, Nathan asked, "How's your swallowing?"

"No problems," his father replied. "That speech pathologist gal came to check on me yesterday. Sharp cookie. I would've hired her to work in my practice. She knows how to work with patients."

"How so?" Nathan asked. He heartily agreed with his father's assessment after having watched Trish work with her father Monday evening, but he wanted to know how his dad saw it.

His father eyes brightened and met Nathan's. "She doesn't talk down. She's on the level. You trust someone like that. It's what a good employee is all about."

Nathan thought about his outburst at Gracie and Estevan earlier in the day. After talking to Foster, he'd spent some time apologizing to them and trying to explain his concerns. How they needed to really work as a team. Estevan tried to shrug it all off as a 'stress mess,' but Gracie remained uncharacteristically silent during the meeting, and her eyes were evasive. Nathan could see that she was hurt, and his apology and explanation had not healed her.

"Did you ever have to fire anyone?" Nathan asked his father.

Dr. Danforth nodded. "Twice. Wasn't fun, but sometimes people aren't a good fit. They can't be trusted to keep their promises." He looked away from Nathan, lowering his head. "I couldn't save your mother or the Orchard."

Nathan was thunderstruck by his father's admission, the hint of self contempt.

"You didn't fail," he told his father. "I wouldn't be here without you. You're not responsible for what happened to Mom or the Orchard. You've given Garrett and me so much, and we are here for you always. I hope you believe me, Dad."

His father did not answer. His thin hand reached for the television remote and unmuted the TV set. A national news anchorman was going on about turmoil in the Middle East.

"What's wrong with the world?" his father asked absently.

What's wrong with us? was the only response that came to Nathan's mind.

Bleary eyed, Nathan poked at his oatmeal as Jillian poured him a cup of coffee.

"You look a bit down-in-the-mouth, honey. Didn't you sleep well?" she asked.

"Not great. Too much on my mind. Between Dad and that Sunset Gardens contract my mind is in the middle of a giant tug-o-war."

She handed him the cream for his coffee. "Sorry to hear that, sweetie. I sure wish I could change all that for you."

"Yeah, I wish these gold coins were 'magic beans' instead!" as he stirred the cream into his coffee.

"Say, do you think you'll be able to make it to Lisa's teacher conferences tonight? It's okay if you can't. I can go myself."

Rubbing his temples, Nathan replied, "Sorry. I'd forgotten all about it. I should be able to go, though. It's important to check in with her teachers."

"Particularly with her English teacher," Jillian said. "Lisa said they aren't exactly seeing eye-to-eye."

"What's the problem?"

"Lisa doesn't think he likes the way she writes. She says he grades her essays really hard."

"Is she failing the class?" he asked.

"No. No. She's got a B, but she wants an A."

"That's the spirit. I like that attitude," Nathan said. "Plan on me going with you, unless the sky falls—or Amazon calls for windows in their new campus downtown."

Jillian laughed. "Good. And by the way, and not to add to your worries, but we got the cable bill yesterday and the rates went up." She held her hands up as Nathan frowned. "I forgot to tell you last night, and you said you always wanted to know when they raised their rates, so you could call to threaten to cancel unless they come down in price."

Nathan banged his coffee cup on the table. "They play such a game. Raising your rates every five or six months and then if you call threatening to cancel, they find some special promotion to keep you at the same rate. I hate that."

"Then why don't we change providers. There are alternatives to cable. We could try a satellite service—or we could be daring and go 'off the grid.'" Jillian suggested.

"All those companies play the same game. And as for going off the grid, I'd do it, if I wasn't such a sports junkie. I've got to feed my habit, you know?"

"Then you better play the cable company's game. The piper must be paid."

Nathan rolled his eyes. "Why does this feel like it's going to be long day?"

"Probably because you had a long night. Want another cup of coffee?"

Nathan had already had two cups of coffee; still he stopped on his way into work for a third. However, he didn't go to Seven Coins. He stopped in at Starbucks instead. The place he'd gotten his coffee for years. The shop Annette was competing head-to-head with. He wanted to see if there really was a difference, or if was just the novelty of it.

It was a little after seven and already the Starbucks was packed. Three baristas worked the espresso machines and two more took orders and rang customers up. It was crowded, but orderly. Everybody knew the drill. Folks in line smiled and chatted, the baristas did too – as much as they could with it being so busy. It had a warm and comfortable feeling in the shop. Familiar. Nathan got his latte. It was good. It was routine. It was what he expected. But no more.

As he exited, he noticed the Starbucks mission statement etched into the wall to the left of the fireplace. *'Our mission is to inspire and nurture the human spirit – one person, one cup, and one neighborhood at a time.'*

Were the gold coins in his pocket creating unreal expectations? Did he have to analyze every transaction for some deeper meaning? That seemed senseless. Sometimes a cup of coffee *was just a cup of coffee*. If you enjoyed it, it was worth it.

He got in his car and drove past Seven Coins as he left the strip mall. How could Annette expect to compete with Starbucks in the long run? Her coffee was good, a bit better than Starbucks, but it was also a little more expensive. It'd be easy for Nathan to start going back to Starbucks, forget about Annette's five remaining gold coins in his pocket, and just soldier on at Winning Windows.

It'd be easy.

Maybe.

But Nathan wasn't that naïve. Starbucks had started small, too. One shop. It grew because its reputation grew—and because of an owner who had a vision and could lead others to embrace that vision. Annette had opened a door, made Nathan see some possibility where he hadn't before. Like Annette's coffee shop against Starbucks, Winning Windows couldn't compete head-to-head on price with a bigger manufacturer like AMVIC Windows.

Then, something about standing in line at Starbucks hit him. The baristas were all using machines to make coffee drinks. Push a button and it was done.

That wasn't how Seven Coins Coffee was doing it. They were doing it like Starbucks used to. Starbucks had gone the way of growth—it had automated. The employees were still pleasant and nice, but craftsmanship was being pushed out by efficiency and volume. The drive-thru window was endemic of that.

Nathan didn't think he'd ever see a drive-thru window at Seven Coins. Convenience could easily become code for becoming *impersonal*. It didn't have to be. Nathan had been through a lot of drive-thrus and had good service, but that was more of an assembly line. It was not unlike the debate he'd had about bringing automation to Winning Windows. If Annette was right, automation was not going to make for authentic transactions.

Nathan considered how many fewer interactions he had these days, what with cash machines, swiping his credit card at fuel pumps, self-checkout at all kind of stores, online banking. Convenience. Was that all worth it?

What did face-to-face transactions offer? What did a small business do that a large one could not? A smaller business had to offer something more. Otherwise why was it there? How could it possibly compete?

The question now was, would he let the door quietly shut on that possibility, or would he slam it shut himself? Would he let this be like any other

Thursday morning? He had to find a way to articulate that for himself and his employees.

As he drove along, he realized how much depended on what he believed and what he was willing to do. So much can depend upon one person and he pondered whether or not he was that kind of person.

Twelve years ago he'd bought Winning Windows. Was he the kind of person who could have started it from scratch like Annette had done with Seven Coins Coffee, or his father with his dental practice? Was he the kind of person who could prevent Winning Windows from failure?

His mind was spinning. All these questions, plus a lack of sleep and a confounding dream – not to mention three cups of coffee – had made his mind a whirling centrifuge. Suddenly, flashing lights danced in his eyes. He blinked a few times trying to shake them off before he realized a police car was behind him, trying to pull him over.

A rush of adrenalin snapped him to attention. He put on his blinker and pulled off onto a side street to stop. He'd held out a fleeting hope that the police car just wanted him out of the way, so it could speed to some other emergency. But the police car pulled up behind him and parked.

This is all I need, Nathan thought. Nathan couldn't think of what he'd done to get pulled over. It'd been twenty years since he'd gotten any kind of ticket and he felt flustered.

He scrambled to open his glove box searching for the registration and proof of insurance documents, hoping they were up to date. Once he located them, a glance told him they were current, and he breathed a long sigh of relief. Then he extracted his driver's license from his wallet and waited.

After a few minutes on his cruiser's computer, the officer emerged from his car. He walked around to the passenger side of Nathan's car, looking through the window, and went to the front. He studied it for a moment and then walked to the driver's side.

Nathan had already rolled the window down. "Hello, officer, what's the problem?" he managed.

The officer crouched at the window, so that he was eye-level with Nathan. A square-jawed man who looked to be in his mid-thirties, he quickly scanned Nathan and the interior of the car.

"Driver's license, registration and proof of insurance, please," he said.

Nathan handed them to the officer. He wanted to ask again what he'd done wrong, but he bit back his question, feeling it best to let the patrolman lead this dance.

"Mr. Perkins, where are you going this morning?" the officer asked somewhat casually reading his name off his license.

The question took Nathan off guard. "To work."

"And where would that be?"

"At Winning Windows. It's about a mile down the way, near Canyon Park."

The officer nodded. "Have you come from the vicinity of Maltby?"

"No. My home is south of here in the Kingsgate area."

The officer nodded again. "One moment, please." He returned to his patrol cruiser with Nathan's paperwork.

Again, the wait was excruciating for Nathan. He couldn't for the life of him figure out what he'd done wrong. Driving this route, as he did almost every day, he'd been on automatic pilot. Yes, he'd been thinking about some heavy questions, but he didn't think he'd been speeding or run a red light. The longer he had to wait, the more his anxiety increased, as well as his irritation. It'd been a long time since he'd been pulled over by a cop.

Before he could get any more worked up, the officer was back squatting at his passenger window, handing him back his license and registration and insurance card. "Mr. Perkins, I'm sorry for the inconvenience. We had report of a hit and run near Maltby and your car matched the make, model and color of the suspect vehicle. Again, I apologize for the stop, and I hope I didn't raise your blood pressure too much."

The patrolman's explanation instantly flushed Nathan's anxiety and irritation away. "I understand, officer. That's terrible. I hope you catch the guy."

"We're trying. Thanks again for your cooperation, Mr. Perkins. Oh, and since I took a bit of your time this morning, just a tip on this car. Be sure to have the timing belt replaced when recommended in the service booklet. My brother in-law and another friend own this particular model and both had their timing belts break within a thousand miles of the recommended replacement mileage. That just might be a fluke, but, believe me," the officer offered a friendly grin, "a busted timing belt is an expensive pain in the neck."

Nathan returned his smile. "Thank you, officer. I haven't checked the scheduled maintenance book for a bit. I'll be sure to look into it."

The officer stood up and lightly tapped the top of Nathan's car. "I'll let you get on your way. Drive safely and have a good day."

Nathan was so relieved. He put his license back in his wallet and the other documents in the glove box. Then a thought struck him. He reached into his jacket pocket and took out one of Annette's coins. He hesitated.

Would it be too strange? Could it be construed as a bribe in some odd way?

It'd be awkward, but wasn't that one of Annette's points. Let people know when they've gone over and above in an everyday transaction. Being pulled over by a cop wasn't an everyday thing for Nathan. He'd been dismayed initially, but the officer had done his job very professionally. And then he'd personally recognized Nathan's cooperation and understanding and offered some advice in return.

Both Nathan and the policemen did their duty, but the officer went beyond his. Nathan should do the same. He undid his seatbelt and got out of the car. The officer was just getting into his car when saw Nathan get out of his. He stopped and stiffened as Nathan approached.

"Did I forget to give you something back?" the officer asked.

"No," Nathan answered as he approached. He held out the metal coin with the handshake etched in it. "This may seem silly, but I actually own Winning Windows. A fellow small business owner challenged me to see if I can give out seven of these coins in a week. It's meant to be a symbol of great service in an everyday transaction. Even though I was surprised by being pulled over this morning, I appreciated your professionalism and the tip on the timing belt. I hope you'll accept this as a token of good service."

The officer took the coin. He pretended to bite it. "If it were real gold I'd be worried about a bribe."

Nathan laughed. "That very thought almost kept me from offering it to you."

"No worries," the officer said. "I like the idea behind it. It's not every day, someone thanks me for pulling them over." He held out his hand and Nathan shook it.

"Keep up the good work, officer."

"It's a lot easier when I'm working for folks like you. Have a good day, Mr. Perkins"

"You too."

When Nathan returned to his car, settled in and started the ignition, he felt like he was restarting his whole morning. His head felt clear. His mind was free of worry. He was actually excited about going to work.

Nathan was still beaming as he pulled into the parking lot. But he knew a daunting task waited. Not only did he have to make peace with Gracie and Estevan, but he had to unite them on a strategy for the Sunset Gardens contract. When he got settled at his desk and went back through all the bid information they had put together for him, he still had no clear idea what to do. He spun his wheels for twenty minutes, then decided to tackle another unpleasant task instead.

He called his cable company.

It was so formulaic. So contrived. In his mind, Nathan played out the conversation as if stuck in an abusive relationship:

> ~You hurt me, Comcast. You're beating me down and I don't love you anymore. I'm leaving you for good.
>
> ~I can change. It can be like it was before. Don't leave me. Direct TV can't do what I can for you. Don't you remember all the good times we had?

Forget their promises. Forget what I said and did yesterday. I'm a new man. I'm nothing without you,...until I do the same to you in a few months.

When he finally got through to a 'live' service rep, Nathan tried to cut through the smoke and mirrors, but the guy was locked into a script. He had to follow protocols. He was being monitored. Nathan couldn't really blame him. Yet, by the time he got off the phone and his monthly rate had been restored to what it had been previously by a 'customer loyalty promotion' for another six months, Nathan had had a bit of a revelation.

The rep wasn't free to negotiate. He had a matrix to follow with customers that didn't ultimately serve them; it stalled them. Froze them in place.

Companies know that people generally resist change. Change can be difficult – even if it's a new remote controller and a whole new list of channels and screen interfaces. People like the familiar, the stable. His cable company was banking on that. Literally. Eventually, they'd get their rate hike and couch it in new and better content packages.

Jillian had it right this morning when she'd suggested to him that they should switch providers or "go off the grid." Nathan hadn't wanted to deal with that kind of change. There was risk involved. Not a life-threatening or financial ruin type of risk, but the everyday kind of risk of unpleasant change that could grate on a person's nerves.

Risk. Great or small. It was essential to an authentic transaction. Both sides had to risk something. And that was why trust had to be at the center of a meaningful interaction. A sense of trust was the balancing force to the element of risk.

Nathan could just as well have been talking to an automated recording at the cable company. Automatons couldn't make meaningful transactions. Only people with free will, the power to risk and to trust could. If they felt controlled or tied to someone else's values and agendas, they couldn't establish authentic relationships that were the basis for a meaningful transaction. Nathan had read an article about the online shoe company, Zappos, that their customer service reps actually have the freedom to satisfy the customer as they see fit.

At his desk, Nathan closed his eyes. He realized he'd been trying to steer Gracie and Estevan, make them behave like he thought they should. He'd wanted to control them. Deal with customers exactly like he would.

His father had said something last night when he'd asked him if he'd ever had to fire employees and he had answered that he had. That sometimes people weren't a good fit.

A good fit. It might be with skills and personality. But it also had to do with values. If an employee didn't value what his boss did, that would end poorly. Nathan began to better see Annette's whole idea of going head-to-head with Starbucks and trying to teach her employees with the gold coins. She was living and working her values, calibrating her values with her employees, so she could trust them to make good choices and create meaningful transactions.

It allowed Nathan to envision a way forward with Gracie and Estevan. He needed to reaffirm with them the values of the company. After that, it would be up to them. If they held true to their values that was all he could ask.

They wouldn't get the Sunset Garden account by coming up with an angle. They just needed to be clear. Winning Windows products were very high quality and an excellent long-term value. That belief had to be the foundation they acted upon. They might always risk another company undercutting them on price, but they had to believe in the lasting worth and value of their product. They had to stand by it.

Nathan stood up from his desk, picked up the bid information and walked out determined that, if nothing else, Gracie, Estevan and he could always look each other confidently in the eye when doing business.

Nathan wished Gracie and Estevan both had accepted a gold coin. Then, he would only have two left. Still, he felt grateful that after talking with them they not only understood the message underlying Annette's token, they seemed to embrace it. Gracie, in particular, had latched onto the concept.

"This is so I can remember the day after I thought about quitting," Gracie told Nathan and Estevan as she affixed the coin to her office door with a drop of superglue. "I was pretty upset with you yesterday, Nathan. We care about this place too. More than you might know."

"Well," Nathan responded, pointing at the coin on the office door, "this will be a reminder for me, as well, to trust your judgment."

"Mine more than his," Gracie said gesturing to Estevan.

"Sure, Miss Amazing Gracie," Estevan teased, and Nathan knew they were back as a team.

Their meeting had lasted almost two hours. Two hours of being truthful, listening. Nathan had always thought Gracie and Estevan never listened to each other, but they did. They just had a very different way of doing it. And, they listened to him as he explained his core values of *integrity, honesty, respect, hard work, communication* and, ultimately, *quality* and *service*. Nathan wanted Winning Windows to always be centered on outstanding quality and top-notch service.

Gracie and Estevan listened. And they agreed that those values were essential, though they asked Nathan to include *teamwork* and *trust* among the company's core values. He did. It was a good list.

In the two hour conversation, they held to their core values and were honest. Nathan admitted he should've trusted them more. That he should've reached out more to them and other employees to give input on the direction of Winning Windows. He'd mistakenly felt that it was his job, and his job alone, as the owner to set the company's direction. It was his responsibility to get the course set, but that he didn't have to do it alone. Foster had seen that. Why hadn't Nathan?

For his part, Estevan acknowledged that he should've been the one to tell Gracie about rolling her eyes when customers seemed indecisive. Gracie admitted she didn't know she was doing it and wished someone had told her earlier. At that point, they promised to stop bickering and Nathan had laughed. "Fat chance. That's how you guys operate. Just be aware that not everyone knows you as well as your co-workers."

"We can be more professional – especially around customers," Estevan promised.

"But don't sacrifice your personalities," Nathan responded. "I just need people who hold the same values that underlie what Winning Windows is and can be. A list of values won't solve all our problems or challenges, but it'll help us get grounded in the same beliefs. And trust our judgment when we make company decisions."

"That's why I was so upset yesterday," Gracie had acknowledged. "That lack of trust. That feeling that you didn't respect my judgment – or personality. That hurt."

It made Nathan realize that a transaction could be a long process. And, potentially, a treacherous one. He'd been focused on simple transactions like getting his daughter's tire fixed at the tire shop or his unsatisfying interaction with the cable company earlier. Deeper transformational transactions took time. He needed to remember that. More investment, more risk – but the payoff could be much greater.

That was why Nathan presented Gracie and Estevan the gold coins. For the risks they'd taken in their meeting. For their honesty, for listening. For hearing him out and working through the values process. It had been a meaningful transaction. One that had started poorly when he'd blindsided them with criticism the day before. Only their willingness to come back together, communicate, reaffirm the company's core values and move forward with a clear purpose had salvaged the transaction. They'd agreed on what Winning Windows stood for and should always strive for.

Nathan had offered one of Annettes' coins to each, but Estevan had remained adamant, "Just one, please. We're a team. We did this together."

As Nathan walked up the stairs to his office, he was no longer worried about Sunset Gardens. Gracie and Estevan knew what was at stake and what to do. They were scheduled to meet with Mike Corbin, the Sunset Gardens' contractor, tomorrow morning and make their case. It was going to be straightforward: in terms of quality, style and the cost of ownership when energy savings were included, Winning Windows would stand by their products as the best long-term value in the region. Even though AMVIC Windows might quote a lower up-front cost, in the long run, their windows were superior in every way. *That* they could promise with complete confidence.

"Sounds like you've had quite the day – and week," Jillian said as they finished up dinner. It was just Nathan and her. Lisa was working at the mall. Nathan had filled her in on his eventful day and the effect Annette's gold coins were having on the way he was thinking about everyday – and not so everyday – transactions.

"Let's see," she recounted. "You got pulled over as a potential hit-and-run driver, and then you pulled together your sales team to save the company. And all because of some magical coins an upstart coffee-brewing business guru gave you. I think I need to see one of these coins."

Nathan retrieved one from his jacket pocket. "Careful. In the wrong hands these might be dangerous."

"I'll risk it," Jillian said, taking a look at the coin. "So, do you think I'll earn one of your special coins?"

"What kind of transaction are you offering?" Nathan asked with a knowing smirk.

Jillian flung her hair back behind her shoulder and tilted her head flirtatiously with her best come-hither eyes. "How about I clean up the dishes while you take out the trash? Is that a satisfying enough transaction for the man with the golden coins?"

Nathan laughed. "Good enough for now. Hey, when do we have to be at school for the teacher conferences?"

"About ten minutes ago."

Nathan stood up alarmed. "Shouldn't we get going then?"

"Relax, honey. They always start with that parent overview which we've heard before. Then the conferences start. Remember? They're arena-style. We wait in line for ten or fifteen minutes and then get five minutes with the teacher. I figure we'll split up to see most of Lisa's teachers and then go together to see her English teacher. That's the class she's most concerned about."

"Sounds like a plan," Nathan agreed as he got up from table to go get ready.

Twenty minutes later they were being greeted in the high school gym by the school's counselors handing out student schedules. Nathan and Jillian looked over Lisa's.

"Why don't you go talk to her pre-Calculus and Business Law teachers. I'll go see her Spanish and

Chemistry teachers," Jillian suggested. "Then we'll meet at her English teacher, Mr. Kline, and talk to him together."

She gave him a kiss on the cheek and headed off to find the line for Lisa's Spanish teacher.

Fortunately for Nathan, the lines to see Lisa's pre-Calc and Business Law teachers were not very long. But, then, neither were the conferences. Both teachers were organized and pleasant. Each obviously knew Lisa well and each dutifully showed Nathan a progress report of all her assignments. She was getting an 'A' in both classes. Both her pre-Calc and Business Law teachers encouraged Nathan to call or email if he had any concerns and handed out a standard-looking form that had their contact information, as well as the school's website where they had class information, assignments and tests posted. All very efficient and generic. To the teachers, Lisa was a model student and she just needed "to keep doing what she was doing."

Her Business Law teacher did comment that Lisa might make a good lawyer because she was "very assertive" and a "good advocate for herself." Nathan tucked those gems away to ask Lisa when they got home. He wondered if Lisa and the teacher might have had a bit of disagreement about something in the class. He knew how strong-willed his daughter could be. She liked to question rules that made no sense to her.

After his two routine conferences, Nathan found Jillian waiting in line to talk to Lisa's Chemistry teacher. "How'd your chats go?" she asked.

"Fine," Nathan responded. "Our daughter is a model student as you know."

"Certainly. But wouldn't it be nice if she could keep her clothes off the floor in her room."

"Pick your poison, dear."

Jillian sighed. "I guess I'd rather have a model student with a messy room, than a neatnik who was flunking out."

"See. It's all about perspective," Nathan reassured. "I'm going to go get in Mr. Kline's line. It's one of the longest. I guess lots of parents want his perspective on their kids. I'll see you there when you finish here."

"Will do," Jillian said.

She joined him in line ten minutes later. "Good timing," Nathan remarked. Only one set of parents was in front of him.

"So how do you want to handle this?" Jillian asked.

"Let's just see what Mr. Kline has to say first."

He had a lot to say. Immediately after standing up to greet them, he shuffled through some folders and brought out some of Lisa's written work.

"I think Lisa would like to poke my eyes out with the red pen I use to grade essays," Mr. Kline joked as he spread out her work before them.

"She's mentioned that," Jillian said.

"Poking out my eyes!" Mr. Kline exclaimed in mock astonishment.

Jillian laughed. "Not exactly, but she did mention that she doesn't think you like her writing."

"That's the thing about writing. It's very personal, so when someone critiques it, it can feel like an attack on your character. Fundamentally, Lisa is a sound writer. She knows how to construct a solid essay and lead the reader through it. Good structure and organization."

"I think I hear a big 'but' coming," Jillian interjected.

"*A big 'but'* sounds a bit salacious for public schools, but nevertheless, your intuition is correct. Lisa could certainly benefit from a deeper level of analysis in her essays. That's where I want to see her push herself. I'd wager up until now, she's probably always done well in English because her prose is clear and easy to read."

Both Nathan and Jillian nodded.

"Now," Mr. Kline continued, "just because Lisa is in my Honors class I don't assume she is planning to attend college, and really it makes no difference. I want every student to get better in my class. They all deserve a year's worth of growth. All students need to up their intellectual game as they get closer to graduation. With Lisa, I'd like to try to sharpen her thinking through her writing. She's great at synthesizing what we've discussed in class, and now she needs to take a few more risks with her own ideas. Try out some of her own insights and create some of her own original connections to the literature."

"How do *you* help her do that?" Jillian asked, the implication clear.

"I let them fail miserably," Mr. Kline deadpanned. "It sounds awful, but, at some point with their writing and thinking, you've got to push them out of the nest and get them flapping their wings. It's seldom graceful, but if they believe I'll provide them a relatively soft landing, they begin to be more trusting."

"What about her grade?" Jillian asked.

Mr. Kline frowned. "We have such a confused system. Instead of being focused on what they are learning, most students get distracted by what their grade is going to be. I get that, but it's so counterproductive. Part of our education system's misguided legacy of sorting students to weed out the ones that were not college worthy. If it's only grades we focus on, then we lose too many learning opportunities. Especially the kind that will help Lisa grow as a writer – and a thinker. If she's willing to take some risks with her writing, I can guarantee you that her grade won't be an issue."

Somewhat astonished, Jillian stared back at the Mr. Kline for a few moments. Then asked, enthusiastically, "What can *we* do to help?"

Mr. Kline smiled wickedly, "Tell her to make my pompous fool's eyes bleed with outrageous assertions and notions. Tell her to lay it on thick and give me what I've asked for and more – and then see if I know what to do with it. Most importantly, conspire with me to have your daughter dare the extraordinary."

Jillian laughed. "Are you for real?"

"Only from 7:00 AM to 4:00 PM on weekdays. In the evenings and on weekends, I'm just idealistic."

Jillian locked her eyes on Nathan's. "Give him one of those coins."

Nathan took one from his jacket pocket and handed it to Mr. Kline who looked it over curiously.

"My first attempt at a bribe today! But usually it's from students." he laughed.

Nathan took a minute to explain the significance of the coin to Mr. Kline.

"Better than a bribe, a pact," Mr. Kline said, reaching across the table to shake Nathan and Jillian's hands. "I look forward to sharing this with my colleagues."

"Just don't tell Lisa," Nathan warned. "She'll think we're nuts."

"But that's just what you have to be to grow," Mr. Kline advised, letting the metaphor sink in.

"Three coins yesterday?" Annette's eyebrows lifted in astonishment. "If you've got a few minutes, let me take care of the folks behind you and then I'd like to hear about these transactions."

"Sure," Nathan said, as he picked up his chocolate-pumpkin latte, a treat for himself this Friday morning for what had been, at times, a challenging week. He was feeling good, though. He sipped on his latte and watched Annette and her baristas bantering with customers. For the most part, they knew each customer's name.

At Seven Coins, the employees looked to be working hard to know their customers by sight. That was impressive. So, when Annette made her way over to Nathan, he complimented her on her barista's prowess with names.

"I tell them that learning a customer's name is always the first step to employee superstardom," Annette agreed. "Customers always like coming back to a place they're known. It's simple, and it pays big dividends on a personal and professional level."

"You aren't running a coffee shop here, Annette. You've built a business school lab, and your employees are getting paid in both dollars and retail sense."

Annette smiled. "From day one, I've told you I had ulterior motives."

"Changing the world was one, I believe," Nathan remarked.

"Exactly, but I didn't think you'd become one of my evangelists quite so quickly. By my count, you've given away five coins in four days. You must think I'm made of fake gold, Mr. Perkins."

"At the outset, I honestly wasn't sure I'd give away any. It seemed a bit hokey when you first told me about it. But, looking for meaningful transactions with an authentic give and take between folks has opened my eyes."

Annette nodded. "Amazing what happens when you focus on something. It's like that thing suddenly expands. It's like bird watching. Something I've recently dabbled in. A year ago, couldn't have told you if there were any birds around my house and neighborhood. But, once I became interested in birds, I found that there was quite an extensive avian population literally at my doorstep. And it gets richer and deeper at every glance."

Annette paused and took a drink of her coffee. "So, once you start looking closely at something – whether birds or transactions – it opens up that world. Hopefully, for the good. Now tell me about your transactions from yesterday."

Nathan started with being pulled over by the patrolman and how considerate the officer was of Nathan being inconvenienced. He explained what happened with Gracie and Estevan. Annette was quite interested in that interaction and told Nathan those were the kind of moments that sometimes could make or break a business. She congratulated him on how he'd handled it. Finally, he told her about the parent/teacher conference with Lisa's English teacher and that, technically, he did not give away that gold coin. Jillian had.

Annette enjoyed hearing that. "Your wife sounds like one sharp woman. I like her already. I hope you bring her by sometime."

"I will," he promised. "At first, she called them 'magic coins' as a joke, but I think she sees they do have a certain power – if only to wake us up to what goes on between people every day."

"Indeed. There is power in that," Annette said. "Two left. At this rate, you shouldn't have any problem meeting your quota by Monday."

"I dunno. That's the kind of statement that seems to jinx things," Nathan warned.

She smiled knowingly. "That's only if you believe in jinxes."

Unfortunately, Nathan did.

An hour after Nathan got to his office, Garrett called. "I'm sorry, Nathan, but we can't take Dad tomorrow. Beth's come down with a nasty bug, and I think I'm getting it, too."

"Is Beth okay?"

"It's an upper respiratory thing. First, a sore throat and then a lot of dripping and hacking. I'm getting the sore throat, so neither of us should be around Dad."

"No doubt."

"Can you call him or go see him this evening to tell him we won't be able to go?" Garrett asked. "I know he'll be disappointed."

"Maybe not. I think Jillian and I can manage it. We won't plan on staying as long, but I think it would be good to get him out to the Orchard." Nathan thought about the serene far-away look he'd seen in his father's eyes the other night. "He was really looking forward to it. We can handle it."

"I hate to put that burden all on you. You know he can be a handful if he gets worked up about something."

No one knew that better than Nathan. "That's true, Garrett, but I think it's worth the risk. Dad needs this. We'll take good care of him."

"Well, if you're willing to try, that's great. Be sure to let me know how it goes. And, if my sore throat is gone by tomorrow morning, I'll come along."

"No worries. You take care of yourself and Beth. I'll give you a call tomorrow afternoon and fill you in on how it went."

"Thanks, Nathan. Dad will really appreciate getting out there."

Yeah, Nathan thought, *but where will it really take him?*

Gracie and Estevan came into Nathan's office late that Friday afternoon with the news. Mike Corbin from the Sunset Gardens project hadn't accepted their bid. Mike had said Winning Windows units were too expensive, and that unless they could lower their price by 15%, he would go with AMVIC Windows.

"He tried to get that 15% out of us this morning," Estevan complained. "But we stuck to our guns, showing him that the apartment building owner would recover that 15% within four to five years with the energy savings."

"I'm sorry, Nathan. We couldn't get him to see past the short term," Gracie lamented. She looked crushed. "He said he couldn't wait for any savings. He needed windows now at the budget he'd been given to work with."

Nathan was resigned. "Well, we can't give him that 15%. We'd be selling at a loss and we know our windows are worth it. Right?"

Estevan looked at Gracie and they both looked at Nathan. "We believe that, but we also know the company could really use this business."

"Doesn't matter," Nathan said. "We stick to our values. Besides, that would be a 'bad transaction' for us. Remember, it has to be mutually beneficial. Call Mike up. Thank him for considering us and tell him we understand his reasons for not going with Winning Windows, but we have to stick to our original bid. Just remind him that we offer excellent value and hope we can do business with him on any future projects."

Estevan nodded. Gracie clenched her fists. "The guy's a fool," she spit out.

"No," Nathan said quietly. "His hands are tied, just like ours are. He's got a bottom line, too."

Nathan left the office that evening feeling his company's bottom line had hit rock bottom. Cold, hard bedrock bottom.

Later that night, Nathan dreamed. Standing on the dusty road, his eyes stinging. He searched in vain. His leaden legs would not obey him. Worse yet, he began sinking into the roadbed as if it had become quicksand. And all he could do was flail in ever slower motion.

He tried to shout, but he couldn't. Dread filled him, he struggled to get free and he sunk deeper still.

He lunged as he felt a touch on his shoulder.

"Nathan, Nathan" Jillian was saying. "You okay?"

Nathan slowly oriented himself to his surroundings. He'd thrown off half the covers. "Sorry," he told Jillian. "Bad dream."

She cradled his shoulder. "Do you want to tell me about it?"

'No, that's all right. You go back to sleep. I'll be fine," he lied and gave her a kiss.

Soon he heard Jillian breathing evenly. Nathan knew he should try to sleep, but the dream haunted him. He didn't want to sink into that dusty, nightmarish road.

He needn't have worried. He would never dream of it again.

The Orchard. It was sixty acres of farmland about twenty miles northeast of Woodinville in gently rolling hills. When his father had grown up there in the 1930s and 40s there'd been nothing but other farms surrounding it. Now, it was a bit of an agricultural oasis among the housing developments that had colonized the once bucolic surroundings.

The family that had purchased the Orchard from Nathan's grandparents in the late 1970s had done a remarkable job of transitioning the farm from being solely reliant on the whims of the prevailing produce prices to a semi-tourist destination. The Orchard did a little of everything: always fresh seasonal produce featuring their apples, u-pick strawberries, raspberries and blueberries in the summer, canning and jam-making workshops, wine-tasting events, catered weddings and parties in the orchards or in the remodeled barn, a petting zoo, a beer garden and bands during Oktoberfest, a pumpkin patch, a cider press, a corn maze, Christmas trees and sleigh rides, a coffee shop and bakery in the rebuilt farmhouse – and, of course, the requisite gift shop.

That was the only galling thing to Nathan. The gift shop. When his father had first seen it over a decade ago, he'd reacted like someone had built a Wal-Mart in the middle of the Grand Canyon.

Nathan understood it was the price for the Orchard's plush acreage not being turned into another subdivision, so he didn't begrudge the high-end crafts and knick-knacks and over-priced gardening equipment. The gift shop abutted the Orchard's extensive produce market in a newer building near the large gravel parking lot the owners had added in the 1990s when the Orchard had become a local destination.

Luckily, Nathan could bypass the gift shop and park on the far side of the pond that bordered the south end of the Orchard. The pond was part of the wetland area that had wooden boardwalks and hard-packed gravel trails linking into the Orchard's trails and apple tree-dotted meadows.

On this late Saturday morning, favor was shining on them, too. The weather was as predicted. Clear and not too cold. In fact, in the bright sunlight, it was quite comfortable. And, in spite of his ominous dream and having slept poorly, Nathan was pleased at how well it had gone so far. When he and Jillian had shown up at his Aurora apartment, Dr. Danforth

Perkins was waiting in a tweed jacket and tie with a wool overcoat and fedora in his hands.

Nathan had worried how his father would react to the news that Garrett and his wife were not coming, but he'd brushed past it. "Too bad. Looks to be a beautiful day." Jillian had looked at Nathan in wonder. And the wonder continued on the drive out to the Orchard. His father was almost chatty. He pointed to various landmarks giving some history and lamented over some newer buildings and what they'd replaced. Jillian encouraged his reminiscences as Nathan drove.

By the time they'd parked by the pond and started to make their way along the path that led up through the lower apple orchard, Nathan was optimistic about the day. Yesterday had been such a letdown: the failure of getting the Sunset Garden contract and the trepidation of taking his father to the Orchard without Garrett and Beth.

But, so far so good. His father could be unsteady at times on his feet, and he did not like to use a walker. Nathan and Jillian had planned to walk on either side of him and offer support, but he was not having any of that – and he didn't seem to need it.

Nathan hadn't seen his father so sure footed in years. Danforth walked slowly, yet steadily, up through the lower orchard, pausing from time to time to look back at the pond, occasionally crossing to pat a tree trunk or tug on a lower limb. It was like he was saying hello to old friends he hadn't seen in a long time.

"Used to climb these old puppies every day," his father touted. "Wish I still could."

Jillian took his arm. "I don't know, Doctor. You're looking pretty spry today. You might still be able to."

"Don't go encouraging him," Nathan joked. "He's part squirrel, according to the stories Grandma Perkins used to tell."

Nathan detected what might be a smile on his father's face. "That'd only be because she fed us rodent from time to time," Danforth said. "She called it her 'surprise stew.' The only surprise was on the part of a few squirrels, I imagine."

Jillian laughed. "This place must fill you with memories." She breathed deep. "What marvelous weather."

Danforth nodded and headed to the upper orchard where the barn and main house were located. A couple of children came racing towards them with their parents behind calling to them to slow down. Nathan watched his father's eyes follow the children down the path, as he tipped his hat to the parents.

They meandered through the upper orchard and when they came to the big cedar-sided barn, instead of going into it, Dr. Danforth moved around the side with Nathan and Jillian following close behind. In the thick grass wet with dew, he made his way carefully to the far corner of the barn. He seemed to be searching the roughly cemented stones that served as the barn's foundation. At the very corner, his eyes widened the faintest bit and he pointed to a triangular stone.

"See that?" he asked. "Look close and you'll see my initials. Cut 'em into that stone when I was six or seven. It was a darn hot summer day, and I was killing time in the shade before ma found more chores for me to do."

Nathan squatted down and traced the initials: DNP. "Danforth Nathaniel Perkins," he announced. "That'd be you."

His father nodded and then set off, but not back the way they'd come. In fact, there wasn't any path at all, just a grassy field that rose slowly to a knoll peppered with brawny old oaks.

"Where you going, Dad?" Nathan asked surprised and a little concerned.

"I want to see something," he replied continuing to move carefully.

"Where?"

"Up by those trees," his father replied, gesturing towards the top of the knoll.

Nathan stepped closer and took his arm. "Hang on, Dad. I don't know if that's a good idea. It's not that steep, but it might be slick. Your shoes will get all wet, and we don't want you to fall."

"Then stay close," Dr. Danforth commanded.

Jillian took his other arm and they slowly inched up the slope. At the top, Nathan could understand why his father had wanted to make the little climb. Looking back down the gentle slope, most of the Orchard was visible: the meadow surrounding the pond, the upper and lower stands of apple trees, the towering barn and farmhouse. All of it bathed in the crisp sunlight of a late October morning.

It was Norman Rockwell perfect. Simple and heartening. The fall colors were electric. Nathan stood at his father's side marveling at how he must perceive the Orchard. His boyhood home. Where all his dreams began. A tingling wave of nostalgia passed through him.

"This is beautiful, Dad."

"Yes. It certainly is." Dr. Danforth's eyes were bright as he stood in the deep grass, transfixed.

After a few minutes, Nathan asked, "Shall we go back down? Maybe have a cup of coffee in the farmhouse."

"Just one more thing," his father said and turned from the panoramic view of the Orchard. He headed into the cluster of oaks dotting the knoll. Nathan gave Jillian a look of concern and then chased after him. "What is it, Dad?"

His father ignored the question and gingerly made his way to the far side of the knoll that overlooked a large parcel of land that was being cleared.

On this side, an oak tree bigger than the rest anchored the knoll. It looked to be sixty feet tall and sprouted muscular, deeply grooved branches as wide as most tree trunks.

His father patted the great girth of the old oak. "I hoped it was still here. Best climbing tree on the property." He motioned to the remains of a few rough planks nailed into the base that over the years had been split and swallowed by the gnarled bark.

Nathan took a closer look, his eyes following his father's to a weighty branch that ran parallel to the edge of the knoll.

"I used to climb this and be higher than everything on the Orchard," Danforth mused. "From there you could see the old trunk road. Nothing but packed dirt at that time. I'd sit there and watch cars and trucks vanish in the dust. Seemed like they were going somewhere important. Made me want to go there, too."

"Well, you made your mark out there, Dad."

His father's voice seemed very faraway and lonely, "Doesn't always feel that way. I didn't do enough and left too much behind. I should've saved the Orchard for you boys."

Imagining his father as a child sitting in the tree overlooking a broad and unbounded horizon filled Nathan with emotion and sudden understanding. His father had been working, establishing his dental practice, putting in long hours to make it successful. To provide for his wife and children. To create possibilities for their future. And it hadn't all worked out as he thought.

Nathan began to grasp the heartache of his father. He'd invested a lifetime in his family. Sacrifice. Hope. Worry. Joy. Disappointment. Triumph. The whole journey. And it was not enough. His father was still traveling a long dusty road of regret.

Nathan had too often seen that as regret in his own accomplishments, his own choice of profession. That had created some of the initial rift in their relationship and the subsequent drift that had made it difficult to communicate and find some balance.

Standing on the knoll overlooking the Orchard and his father's past, he could see the issues much more clearly. He and his dad were on the same path, the same road—and they weren't as far apart as Nathan had once supposed.

Jillian's voice snapped him back into the moment. "You boys ready to stop playing in these damp leaves. I could use a coffee and a scone."

Dr. Danforth nodded, his gaze faraway and serene.

"Yeah, I'm ready," he told Jillian.

Nathan took the crook of his father's arm to lead him back towards the farmhouse where he'd been born and raised, beginning to understand how charged with meaning those simple words were.

Dr. Danforth Perkins had been born at the Orchard in 1933 in the very farmhouse where they now sat having coffee and pastries. But there was little that remained of the farmhouse Danforth would recognize from his youth. Fire had destroyed most of that in the late 1970s. A kitchen fire that got quickly beyond his mother's control and which prompted Danforth's parents to sell the Orchard and move to a retirement home. Because of the fire, the entire house had had to be rebuilt.

The new owners had made the new farmhouse fit with the rest of the property. It sported a large wrap-around porch and plenty of Craftsman-like features, but it was not Dr. Danforth Perkin's childhood house. The entire downstairs had become a coffee and bakery which featured fresh breads and fancy pastries. There was plenty of seating surrounded by quaint country furnishings and a crackling fire.

It was cozy, but it was not the family home. Nathan could see that in his father's eyes as they sipped their coffee. "Not quite like the old place. You think Gram would approve?"

"Doesn't matter. They sold it. I let them." His words were pointed. His mood had soured as they had approached the farmhouse. Nathan thought he might just be wearing out. His stamina had steadily dwindled since his stroke two years ago, and it'd been a physical and emotional day.

Nathan was feeling that he'd been lulled into a false sense of security by his father's early show of energy. Now he calculated that he and Jillian might have to pay the piper for the outing.

He decided to tread lightly, especially since Jillian had borrowed his wallet and slipped down to the produce market to pick up a few things while Nathan and his father finished their coffee.

"Well, it's good they haven't turned the place into another subdivision," Nathan offered.

"I should've bought the place," Danforth insisted.

"You couldn't afford it back when your parents sold it. Besides who would have run the place?"

Dr. Danforth pointed his finger at Nathan. "You could have."

"Me? I couldn't run the Orchard," Nathan countered, surprised by his father's comment. "I love the place, but I never wanted to operate a farm."

"Couldn't be much harder that running a window company," his dad shot back.

Nathan sighed. It took an effort to stay positive, but he tried. "Dad, I know how hard you worked to build your dental practice. You sacrificed a lot for me. I'm grateful. But Garrett is keeping up what you built. It won't be lost. And," Nathan gestured out the window where they could see the old barn and the upper orchard beyond, "the Orchard is still here. We couldn't keep it in the family. But it's still here and it's still a gem."

"Who'll remember it was ours?" his father lamented.

Nathan pictured his father earlier today, patting the apple trees, pointing out his initials in the foundation of the barn and showing them the rungs grafted into the trunk of the old oak he'd climbed in long-ago summers of promise. It suddenly struck Nathan that his father may have wanted to come to the Orchard to say goodbye. That he might be thinking he'd never get back here again.

Nathan put his hand on his father's. He hadn't held his father's hand since he was a kid. It felt cool and paper smooth, his skin taut and almost translucent. "I'll remember, Dad. Garrett will remember. Our wives and children will remember. You'll always have us. Always."

His father looked from their hands to Nathan's face. Slowly he nodded, his eyes turning to gaze out the windows.

The tender moment was broken by a buzz in Nathan's pocket. His phone was vibrating. Planning to turn it off, he slipped it out under the table and glanced down. It was a text from Garrett. He thumbed open the message: *How's it going with Dad?*

Nathan almost laughed. He didn't know how to answer that at the moment. How would he put all that had happened this morning in a text? He decided he'd wait and call Garrett when he got back home. As he began to press the power button, the phone vibrated again.

Another text, but this one was from Gracie. It read: *Urgent. Call.* She was staffing the showroom this Saturday.

Urgent Gracie had texted. That didn't sound good. A fire? A robbery? Nathan's thoughts jumped to the worst, but he didn't want to call Gracie at the table with his father there, and he didn't want to leave him alone. Luckily, Jillian appeared back from the market. She had a bag overflowing with brightly polished apples and a stunning bouquet of cut flowers.

She sat down with a big grin. "I got you some apples to take back and share, Doctor. And I thought these flowers would brighten up your place."

She turned to Nathan, handing him back his wallet. "Oh, and I gave away one of your magical golden coins."

Nathan gave her a look of surprise as he patted his jacket pocket where he'd kept them.

"One was stuck in your wallet, so I think this was meant to be." Her eyes brightened as she explained. "After I picked up the apples and was about to come back here, I passed their flower stall and was stunned by the variety. I commented on the vibrancy of their selection to the gal at the stand and she and I hit it off. We could've talked flowers for hours. Even after I told her where I worked and that we were competitors in a sense, she wouldn't have any of it. She said anytime folks got fresh, colorful and fragrant flowers it was good for everyone in the business.

"'Quality spoils people in a good way,' she told me. She gave me her card, and we're going to meet next week to see how we can get her flowers into my supermarket's floral department. Isn't that awesome? I went to buy a few apples and made a business deal. Don't you think that's a worthy transaction, Nathan?"

He smiled at his wife. "I do. Boy, you're doing all my work for me." He pulled the last coin from his jacket pocket. "Only one more to go."

Dr. Danforth looked at his son and daughter-in-law completely at a loss.

"Jillian, would you try to explain it to Dad?" Nathan asked, noting his father's confusion.

Motioning under the table, Nathan showed her the text from Gracie. She nodded. Nathan excused himself as she launched into an enthusiastic explanation of the gold transaction coins.

Nathan went out onto the porch and called Gracie who picked up on the first ring. "Nathan, you won't believe this!" she began.

He couldn't tell if she was excited or terrified. "What's going on?" he asked.

"Mike Corbin called about twenty minutes ago. He said he'd still love to do business with us on the Sunset Gardens complex, but understood if we couldn't come down 15% in price."

"Did he want us to cut it to 10% or 5%? I thought we told him yesterday that we wouldn't budge. That our windows were a great value at that price. Period."

"We did. He knows we won't budge, and he says on the Sunset Gardens complex he's only got so much money, so he can't afford our windows on that project."

"Then why'd he call?"

Gracie's voice pitched high in excitement, "He has another project. A high end residential development of 110 homes out near the Orchard that's already broken ground. He said he wants to use our windows out there. 110 homes, Nathan!" she squealed.

"He wants to meet and work out the details early next week. Isn't that wonderful! I just had to tell you."

Nathan leaned against one of the porch posts and looked out over the Orchard, the fall colors alive in the noon sunshine. Beautiful. He wondered if the development Gracie was talking about was the clearing he'd seen from the knoll. *Life is such a roller coaster.*

"Gracie, that's awesome. Well done! Call Estevan and let him know and thank him for me. We'll get this contract ironed out and then celebrate with the whole company. This is the shot in the arm we needed."

"It's because you made us stick to our guns and value our values," Gracie reminded him.

"You said it, Gracie. Thanks again for calling with the news. See you Monday."

Before going back in, Nathan looked at the picture windows on either side of the door. He'd designed and built them for the rebuilt farmhouse. He'd told his father that when the place was rebuilt, but his father had probably long forgotten. He thought he might take this opportunity to remind him that he cared about the Orchard. That it meant a lot to him as well.

When he went in and sat back down at the table his father was holding the gold coin. Jillian took one look at Nathan and asked, "What happened?"

"Something good." Nathan's grin widened. "Gracie just got word that we landed a big order.

Better than the Sunset Gardens deal that fell through yesterday."

Jillian gasped. "That's wonderful. I'm so happy for you." She hugged him and gave him a big kiss, then turned Dr. Danforth. "Did you hear that, Doctor? Winning Windows just got a big contract. Isn't that great?"

Dr. Danforth kept turning the coin in his fingers and didn't reply immediately. When he did, his eyes had a glazed look in them. "Gloria told me about this coin."

Nathan winced at the use of his mother's name for Jillian. It was clear he was a bit disoriented, even agitated.

"Do you like the idea behind it, Dad?" Nathan asked. "I think it has real potential to get people thinking about what really good service means."

"I dunno. This seems like just another gimmick," his father said, frowning. "Just like the gimmicks all those dentists who tried to steal my patients used. Offer people free stuff and empty promises to get them in the door and then all they would do is sell, sell, sell. Your teeth need whitening. Caps. Bridges. Gimmicks to upsell their patients. You got to serve people, not sell to them. That's what you missed, Nathan. You became a salesman, not a provider. I thought if I'd taught you anything, it was to serve. That's what I value. That's the only legacy that matters."

He feebly tossed the coin on the table. "It won't make any difference to people who've lost their way." He bowed his head sadly and muttered, "Let's go. I need to get home."

Late Saturday afternoon, Nathan filled Garrett in on all the glorious and gory details of the day, even having to tell his brother about Annette's golden coins and how that had seemed to trigger such a strong reaction from their father.

"So, Dad was kind of losing it there as he tired out," Garrett said, his voice a bit hoarse and raspy from his cold.

"Yeah, he started out so well. But then his mood turned. He was either tired or fed up with me. Probably both."

Garrett tried to reassure him. "I think the two go hand in hand. Don't blame yourself for it. When he gets tired, he gets cranky."

"Yup, and, boy, did he zing me. Said I didn't understand service. That I didn't value what he valued. That I was just a salesman, all gimmicks and no substance. That little gold coin really seemed to set him off."

"I've heard that lecture a few times too. Especially when I first began working with him. I had ideas about how to generate new patients using ads and promos, and he pretty much shut me down on that approach. 'Service is everything' he preached to me. 'Great care will make you loyal customers and their word of mouth will make you more' was his catchphrase. All of it was true, but he could be pretty intense about it."

"*Intense* is a good description of his reaction today. Though, it's ironic. That's what those gold coins are all about. Great service. Authentic interactions. Meaningful transactions. The same kind of values he holds dear. He just doesn't see it that way."

"Yeah, it's frustrating, Nathan. I wish he really understood what you've done with Winning Windows. That contract you got today should've made Dad proud."

"I thought it might." Nathan took a deep breath. "At any rate, Jillian's pleased, and she sure deserves some kind of saintly reward after letting Dad refer to her as Gloria all the way back to Aurora. Nothing like being mistaken for your father-in-law's dead wife to end a memorable outing."

"Well, give Jillian my thanks. And, again, I'm sorry we couldn't help you out on this one."

"Don't worry. The Orchard was beautiful, and we had a great morning with Dad. I'll get over his criticisms. He might not even remember what he said to me. He kind of had that glazed look the last part of the day. I'll drop by to see him tomorrow, since you and Beth are out of commission. I'll see if Lisa can go. You know how seeing one of his granddaughters cheers him up."

"Indeed," Garrett agreed. "We should put Lisa and Marcy in charge of Dad. They've got him wrapped around their teenage fingers."

"And us, too," Nathan reminded. "You and Beth take care. We'll talk soon."

"Thanks again for taking Dad today. Deep down I'm sure he appreciates you and what you've done. Keep the faith, big brother."

"Thanks for the sentiment, Garrett. Bye now."

Nathan hung up. *Faith*. He had faith in his father. He even felt like he understood the pressures he had put upon himself to provide for his family and his regret at not being able to keep the Orchard in the family. No wonder he seemed lost at times.

Lost. Nathan understood now that not following his core values had left him lost and adrift. But, now he felt like he was more anchored, more focused on his family. Taking care of Jillian and Lisa – and his father. He felt reconnected to what was important in his business: quality and service. It could be that simple. Let the rest of the world be complex. He could handle life one look in the eye, one handshake, one touch of the heart at a time.

He let the rough morning with his father go. He and Jillian had a quiet evening watching a romantic comedy. They laughed a lot and, later, Nathan slept dreamlessly through the night.

Early Sunday afternoon when Nathan and Lisa made it over to Aurora Village, Dr. Danforth Perkins looked uncharacteristically disheveled and his eyes had a glazed, faraway look. When he recognized Lisa, though, he brightened noticeably.

"Hi, Grandpa. How are things?" Lisa asked all bubbly.

"Tolerable. Your father worked me hard yesterday."

"So, I heard. Though it sounds like you were wanting to climb some of those apple trees."

Danforth smiled thinly. "If only. What's new with my beautiful granddaughter?"

"Oh, school and the usual." She threw a glance at Nathan. "I guess my parents are conspiring with my English teacher to make my brain grow. You know how adults can be."

Nathan shrugged. "It takes a village, they say."

"Yeah, and I say it's ganging up," Lisa shot back. "You ever feel like that, Grandpa?"

"Every day," he replied with a nod. "They watch you like a hawk around here."

"I know the feeling," Lisa said with a wink. "Did you know I have a job?"

Danforth looked lost for a moment. "Yes. At the mall? Something to do with teddy bears?"

"Yeah, we help kids build them. It's kinda of a popular thing right now. A bit of rip off, too. The bears are pretty cheap, but the clothes and accessories are really expensive."

"Sounds like a gimmick to me," Danforth said, turning his attention from Lisa to Nathan. "Your father knows all about gimmicks. Did he show you his latest? A little gold coin."

"I don't think Lisa's interested in that," Nathan intervened diplomatically. "Let's talk about something else."

"Actually, Mom told me, so that I wouldn't be surprised if my English teacher mentioned it Friday after the parent/teacher conference. I think it's kind of a cool idea. I might even bring it up with my manager sometime. She's always talking about 'super-pleasing' customers. She'd probably like the idea. Believe me, there are plenty of people who don't have a clue when it comes to good service."

"Amen," Dr. Danforth said and shot a glance at Nathan.

Lisa noted the non-verbal exchange. "You guys feuding about something?" she asked.

"Feuding?" Nathan smiled at her use of the word. "You make it sound like we're the Hatfields and McCoys or something. No. We're not feuding."

Lisa scoffed. "Hey, I'm almost eighteen and I don't know who the Hatfields and McCoys are, but I think I know a freeze-out when I see it. I'm in high school and even I've learned no one likes riding the struggle bus. So, get over this. Blood's supposed to be thicker than water and there's that water under the bridge thing. You know, John Lennon, 'give peace a chance' and all that. We're family after all."

Nathan looked closely at his daughter. Startled. Then he looked to his father who was also watching her. Nathan sure hoped Lisa wouldn't drift away from him like he'd allowed his father to. How could he preserve the trust she had in him? How had he lost that relationship with his dad? It was critical to regain that. To meet in the middle... to have a meaningful transaction.

The thought struck him hard. A meaningful transaction. It didn't have to be only in a business setting. Trust and trust. Respect and respect. Love and love. That was the foundation.

Nathan and his father continued to stare at Lisa.

"Did I hit a nerve there? Sorry, but sometimes, you've just got to say it out loud," she continued. "I'm the Facebook generation. We put it out there, for good or for bad. At least it's not bottled up or festering.

Maybe you two should just try saying what's on your mind."

Nathan was dumbfounded. His daughter got it so simply. He and his father needed to, well, have an authentic transaction. Seek to understand one another. Why had Nathan taken so long to get this far down the road? Maybe he'd been the one lost and left in the dust – not his father.

Lisa looked from her father to her grandfather. "Okay. You guys are making this a little awkward, so I'll just step out the door here for a few minutes and then come back and we can have a nice, normal visit. Okay?"

She patted her grandpa on the shoulder and left the apartment. Father and son were left in stunned silence.

The quiet stretched out until Nathan offered, "She's a perceptive girl."

"She's no longer a girl, Nate, that's a woman there," Danforth declared. "Almost grown up. Reminds me how Gloria could cut to the heart of the matter of just about anything."

"Mom could be tough as nails when needed." Nathan agreed. "I know you miss her, Dad."

Emotion swelled as Nathan contemplated a sudden confession. "I know you don't think I was there for her – or you – when she was dying. That I was putting my business first. I'm sorry, Dad. I don't think I had my priorities straight. And I've let us grow apart since then; that's not right."

Danforth focused on his hands. Nathan could see them trembling. "That's on me too some," he admitted. "I couldn't save everything I cared about – your mother or the Orchard. I couldn't make you want my dream either, to take over my practice. Everything was suddenly out of control and I just wanted something solid to hold onto, something I could count on. It was unbearable," he choked.

Nathan took his father's wrist and met his eyes. "How could anyone have tried harder than you did, Dad?"

Danforth looked into Nathan's eyes and spoke softly, "I should've been bigger, Nate. Should've reached out more to you. It's my fault, just like letting the Orchard get sold. I love that place. When we were there yesterday, I thought about my father and what he'd raised me to be. He taught me respect and loyalty. And I thought I had to repay him. I thought you had to repay me."

"I owe you everything, Dad."

"I've asked too much," Danforth continued with a sigh, "and I know I didn't give you enough. I should've saved the Orchard for you and Garrett and your families."

"You've given us plenty."

"A father can't..." Dr. Dansforth Perkins hesitated. "I never gave you and Garrett the time you needed as boys. That's why I always pushed you. A father wants it better for his kids. A father wants it all. But I never gave you enough…of me." Danforth hung his head for a moment. "After Gloria died, I was consumed by my own loss and never really asked for help. I think I just expected you to figure it out and find me. Help me along."

The dream. Nathan thought. His dad had been lost after all, right in Nathan's plain view.

It had taken his daughter Lisa to push them close enough to really see where they stood. With clarity, Nathan finally understood the vastness of the transaction every parent undertakes on behalf of his or her children. It takes a lifetime to complete, sometimes a lifetime to understand.

A few moments later, Lisa cautiously opened the door.

"You guys okay? I don't see any tears – or blood – so I'm assuming it's safe to come back in."

"Sit down, Miss Smartypants," Dr. Danforth demanded, his eyes sharp and bright. "You've done your counseling for the day."

She took a seat at the kitchenette table. "So what are we talking about?"

"Parenthood, "Nathan replied. "It's mystifying, just like teenagers."

"I'm not mystifying," Lisa countered, "I'm just outspoken."

"Well, thanks for speaking your mind. You helped us clear a few things up."

"Great. Now, you can help solve some of the world's less pressing problems for my generation's future like clean energy and water."

Amused, Dr. Danforth surveyed his granddaughter. "So, what *are* your plans for the future? You want to be a dentist?"

"I'm not sure, Grandpa. I want to go to college. Who knows? Maybe I'll become an English teacher to spite Mr. Kline."

"Spite's not the best career motivation. Try happiness," Nathan suggested.

"Happiness is good. I just want to see it going both ways. I'd like any job I do make my customers as satisfied as it makes me."

Dr. Danforth smiled. Gesturing to Nathan with his hand he asked. "You still have one of those gold coins Jillian showed me yesterday?"

"One," Nathan replied.

"Let me see it, please."

A bit stunned by the request, Nathan took it from his pocket and handed it to his father.

Danforth looked over the golden coin with the etched handshake. He handed it to Lisa. "I think you earned this today."

Lisa smiled and took the coin. "On one condition," she asserted. "Only if I see you two shaking hands. And meaning it!"

Nathan reached across the table and clasped his father's hand. His father's grip was surprising in its firmness.

"Deal?"

They looked each other in the eye and shook.

"Deal."

EPILOGUE

One late Sunday morning in early December at Seven Coins Coffee, Garrett and his wife Beth were asking Lisa and her younger cousin Marcy about school. Lisa lamented that everything was beginning to sound like Mr. Kline's English class. Allusions, symbols, hidden meanings, puns and double entendres seemed to be everywhere she looked. Even the name of the Annette's coffee shop.

Annette, who was sitting one table over with Nathan, Jillian and his father, laughed at Lisa's comment.

"I hope I'm not compounding any teen angst for your daughter," she said. "I thought Seven Coins was pretty straightforward, but I guess you can read a lot into what these coins might mean."

Danforth nodded. "I think we read a lot into things. Sometimes too much. And that can cause problems." He snuck in a wink at Nathan before finishing. "If you don't communicate clearly. If you don't reach out and see what's really on someone's mind."

"Well, that's the challenge," Jillian said as she eyed Nathan and his father. "But, Annette, your little symbolic coins helped nudge all our thinking in a new way. Nathan told me that Garrett has handed some of your coins out to his staff to get them thinking about how to better serve their patients. I may even take a few into the flower shop. I don't suppose you or Nathan envisioned that happening two weeks ago when you offered him those seven coins."

Chuckling, Nathan shook his head, marveling that his family had really wanted to meet Annette and try her coffee. "No. I just came in to try the coffee and figure out how this place was going to compete with the Starbucks across the parking lot. Little did I know Annette was plotting a business revolution."

"I'm only trying to sow a few seeds of happiness," Annette demurred.

"Little gold ones," Danforth said. "I told Nathan I thought the coins were just a gimmick, but you've convinced me otherwise." He pointed to his latte. "And this is mighty tasty coffee. A good product and good service is all you really need. You'll do fine."

"It's started well," Annette admitted. "Though, having been a small business owner for many, many years, Dr. Perkins, you know what a commitment it takes to make it in the long haul."

"Yes. Indeed. It's worth it though, if you're willing to take some risks." He gave Nathan a knowing look.

Annette leaned back and smiled. "Sitting here with your family makes me glad I've taken that risk. It reinforces everything I believe about business. That at its core it's about people and building relationships. You have to have heart and take heart to make it meaningful and last."

Nathan lifted his latte and toasted that sentiment. "Here's to success. In every transaction, may it always be our business to be our best!"

FINAL THOUGHTS

There has been lots of focus in the news on the lack of 'customer service' provided by U.S. corporations. While it has been an irritant for many years, decades more likely, lately it has come to a head with recorded customer service representatives exhibiting incoherent and, frankly, mystifying behavior during service calls. Are these rogue reps that have slipped through the training tracks or is the attention to service by major corporations of so little concern? Ron Judd of the Seattle Times writes, "Corporate America has confused the art of talking about customer service with the practice of actually providing it."

The theme of *The Transaction* emerged several years ago after using the 'coin exercise' in a conference to reveal the impact of service and the transaction that occurs between a customer and an employee. What became clear as this story emerged is that we all engage in transactions each and every day and we have the ability to make them all good ones. I realized just how often I stumbled through transactions at grocery stores, drug stores, the Post Office, in the neighborhood. I discovered that it actually requires an active awareness (and perhaps a little self-examination) to engage in these daily transactions more purposefully. We don't zone out on family members or friends, so why do we do it with others?

Why do we regard these daily transactions so lightly and place the responsibility on clerks or cashiers or sales people to step up 'their' game beyond the corporate required scripts to provide meaning to the transaction? Why do we demand they serve us with little effort of reciprocity? Being a customer shouldn't be a passive act. In fact, by increasing our awareness and participating more wholly in every transaction, we give value for value and make a difference in two lives. In an instant!

This fable is not just about good customer service. It was not written expressly for business managers to read, reflect and reimagine their customer service policy or for corporate leaders to be alerted to the black holes in their company brand or image and declare a new future. It is about becoming a partner in your community, on this planet, and giving back as much as you receive, even in short seemingly insignificant transactions like holding a door open for the person behind you. It is about pausing the relentless internal chatter you keep private as you stand in line, waiting for your latte and being aware of the barista behind the espresso machine. It's about impacting lives and improving yours, one transaction at a time.

Chris Creamer

AFTERWORD

Human beings belong to language. And we all, as humans, engage in *transactions* every day. Language and daily transactions are the foundation of our personal expression and reflect quite specifically with every word we utter, what we value. Being conscious of these values and how we treat each other in every transaction is also the basis of great customer service, customer loyalty and contribution to our local communities. It quite literally constitutes the culture inside the business and the brand on the outside.

The standard definition of a 'transaction' is an interaction where goods, services or money is passed from one person to another. But this definition has little to do with the *quality* (or heart) of the transaction, and it is the quality of the transaction that is essential. The quality of every transaction determines the satisfaction and fulfillment for both parties, and ultimately the success of the transaction.

Another definition of a transaction is an equal exchange of *value for value*. But there has got to be more to a transaction than the exchange of money for a service or item. There has got to be a greater recognition of you as a person, as a human being, as someone other than some 'thing.' There has got be some greater value beyond the exchange itself.

Truly valuing the other person in an exchange is the gateway to service. When you are in service, you willingly acknowledge and appreciate the other person. When you are in service, you are aware of the other person's needs, not just in a physical world, but on an emotional level as well.

A transaction without being 'in service' is shallow, mechanical, void of recognition and appreciation of the other person. Great sales people know that in any effective transaction, relationship is critical and fundamental. The most direct route to generating a powerful relationship in any transaction is in serving the other person.

The Transaction is about exchanges that are value for value, where service moves in both directions as an essential element. There is no room for passivity in daily transactions, because to do so reduces your influence on humankind and your contribution to your community. You may never find a cure for cancer or the common cold, but you can influence the lives of thousands of people. This book will illustrate how authentic transactions enhance the exchange as well as leave each party more fulfilled.

Dr. Marc Cooper, President & Founder
The Mastery Company

SAHALIE PRESS
PO Box 1806
Woodinville WA 98072
sahaliepress@gmail.com

www.ingramcontent.com/pod-product-compliance
Lightning Source LLC
Chambersburg PA
CBHW021406170526
45164CB00002B/525